ANTIGUA AND BARBUDA TRAVEL GUIDE

2024 Edition

Discovering Paradise: Uncover the Hidden Gems and must visit destinations of the Caribbean Twin Islands

By

Roy McKean

TABLE OF CONTENT

CHAPTER FOUR

NAVIGATING ANTIGUA AND BARBUDA

CONCLUSION

DISCLAIMER

Welcome to our immersive travel guide! As you embark on this journey through the pages of Antigua and Barbuda travel guide, we want to set clear expectations. While we aim to transport you to captivating destinations and provide valuable insights, we do so without the aid of maps and images.

Why, you ask?

Our intention is simple: to stimulate your imagination and curiosity. By omitting maps, we encourage you to rely on your instincts, engage with locals, and discover hidden gems beyond the well-trodden paths. Instead of images, we invite you to paint vivid mental pictures through words and descriptions, allowing your mind to craft its unique interpretation of the places we explore.

In this text-centric guide, we prioritize storytelling, history, culture, and practical advice. We believe that your own perceptions and interpretations will make your travels more personal and memorable. It's an invitation to be present in the moment, to interact with your surroundings, and to embrace the serendipitous adventures that come your way.

So, as you delve into these pages, let your imagination soar, and let the words be your compass in this world of exploration and discovery.

INTRODUCTION

Welcome to Antigua and Barbuda

Renowned as the Heart of the Caribbean, Antigua and Barbuda extend a captivating invitation to travelers, showcasing a seamless fusion of natural splendor, storied history, and lively culture. Beyond the postcard-perfect turquoise waters and pristine beaches synonymous with the region, these twin islands unravel a narrative that goes beyond the surface. The warmth of the welcome is more than a sunlit greeting—it's an embrace from the locals, an invitation to delve into the secrets of this Caribbean haven. Step ashore and discover not only the breathtaking landscapes but also the tales embedded in colonial landmarks, the rhythms of vibrant festivals, and the genuine hospitality that makes Antigua and Barbuda an unparalleled destination for those seeking an authentic Caribbean experience.

Why Antigua and Barbuda?

Amidst the vast expanse of the Caribbean archipelago, Antigua and Barbuda stand out as gems awaiting discovery. What sets these twin islands apart, drawing visitors from around the globe?

1. Diverse and Enchanting Landscapes:

Antigua, the larger of the two, boasts 365 beaches, one for each day of the year, each with its own unique charm. From the iconic Pink Sand Beach in Barbuda to the dramatic cliffs of Devil's Bridge in Antigua, the landscapes vary from one breathtaking vista to another.

2. Historical Tapestry:

Steeped in a rich history, the islands showcase remnants of their colonial past. Nelson's Dockyard, a UNESCO World Heritage site, is a living testament to Antigua's naval history, while Betty's Hope, an 18th-century sugar plantation, reveals the economic foundations of the islands.

3. Vibrant Culture and Festivals:

Antigua and Barbuda's culture is a lively fusion of African, British, and West Indian influences. Visitors have the chance to immerse themselves in the rhythm of local life, especially during festivals like Carnival, which pulsates with vibrant parades, music, and traditional dance.

4. Exquisite Culinary Experiences:

The islands offer a culinary journey that mirrors their diverse heritage. Local markets burst with fresh produce and spices, while seaside shacks serve up authentic Caribbean flavors. Visitors can savor the taste of the islands through dishes like pepper pot, fungi, and conch salad.

5. Water Adventures Abound:

Antigua and Barbuda's aquamarine playground beckons water enthusiasts. Whether it's sailing around the coastline, snorkeling in crystal-clear waters, or diving to explore vibrant coral reefs, the islands offer a myriad of aquatic activities for all levels of adventurers.

6. Exclusive Retreats and Luxury Resorts:

For those seeking a touch of luxury, Antigua and Barbuda offer an array of exclusive retreats and world-class resorts. From beachfront villas with private pools to spa experiences that blend local traditions with modern indulgence, the islands cater to the discerning traveler.

7. Barbuda's Pristine Seclusion:

Barbuda, the quieter sister island, captivates with its untouched beauty and tranquil atmosphere. Visitors can escape the hustle and bustle, basking in the serenity of pink sandy beaches and exploring the untouched natural reserves like the Frigate Bird Sanctuary.

8. Warm Hospitality:

The heart of Antigua and Barbuda lies in the warmth of its people. Locals, proud of their islands, readily share stories, recommendations, and genuine smiles. The welcoming spirit extends beyond the touristic spots, creating an authentic connection with every visitor.

9. Adventure Awaits:

Beyond the idyllic beaches, Antigua and Barbuda offer a playground for adventure seekers. Hike to the summit of Signal Hill for panoramic views, embark on a zip-lining journey through the rainforest, or explore hidden caves along the coastline—each moment promises an adventure waiting to be embraced.

CHAPTER ONE

PLANNING YOUR ANTIGUA AND BARBUDA ADVENTURE

1.1 Setting Your Travel Goals

Embarking on a journey to Antigua and Barbuda requires thoughtful consideration and planning, and it all begins with setting clear travel goals. Your travel goals serve as the compass guiding your exploration of these captivating Caribbean islands. Here are essential aspects to consider when defining your travel goals for an unforgettable Antiguan and Barbudan experience.

First and foremost, introspect about your interests and desires. What aspects of travel do you find most fulfilling? Are you an avid history buff, craving a deep dive into the cultural tapestry of these islands? Perhaps you're a nature enthusiast, yearning for outdoor adventures amid lush landscapes and pristine beaches. By identifying your passions, you lay the foundation for crafting a tailor-made itinerary.

Consider the pace of your journey. Are you seeking a leisurely escape, immersing yourself in the laid-back Caribbean lifestyle? Or does your heart yearn for an action-packed adventure, with every day filled with thrilling activities and exploration? Determining the tempo of your trip ensures that you'll find the perfect balance between relaxation and excitement.

Explore the type of experiences that resonate with you. Antigua and Barbuda offer a diverse range of activities, from water sports and hiking to historical tours and cultural events. Whether you dream of sailing along the coastline, discovering ancient landmarks, or simply unwinding on pristine beaches, your travel goals should align with the unique offerings of these twin islands.

Consider the duration of your stay. Are you planning a quick getaway or an extended holiday? Understanding the time constraints allows you to prioritize activities and destinations, ensuring you make the most of your time in Antigua and Barbuda.

Closely related to this is the consideration of the travel companions accompanying you. If you're traveling with family, friends, or as a couple, it's essential to factor in everyone's interests and preferences. Striking a balance between individual desires ensures that each member of your party has a fulfilling and enjoyable experience.

Delve into the cultural and historical aspects of Antigua and Barbuda. Are you fascinated by the colonial history, eager to explore the remnants of sugar plantations and historic forts? Alternatively, you might be drawn to the vibrant local culture, eager to savor authentic Caribbean cuisine, attend local festivals, and interact with the friendly locals.

Research the seasonal highlights of Antigua and Barbuda. Each time of the year brings its own unique charm, from the lively festivities of Carnival to the quieter, more reflective moments during the off-peak season. Aligning your travel goals with the seasonal nuances ensures you capture the essence of these islands at its best.

1.2 Choosing the Best Time to Visit

Selecting the ideal time to visit Antigua and Barbuda is a pivotal decision that can significantly shape your overall travel experience. The islands, situated in the heart of the Caribbean, boast a tropical climate, ensuring warm temperatures and ample sunshine throughout the year. However, nuances in weather patterns and tourist seasons warrant careful consideration when planning your journey.

High Season (December to April):

The high season, spanning from December to April, is characterized by dry and pleasant weather, making it the most popular time for tourists to visit Antigua and Barbuda. During these months, the islands experience lower humidity, minimal rainfall, and temperatures ranging from the mid-70s to mid-80s Fahrenheit (24-29 degrees Celsius). The dry conditions create the perfect backdrop for water activities, beach outings, and outdoor adventures.

This peak season aligns with the winter months in the Northern Hemisphere, attracting visitors seeking an escape from colder climates. Consequently, the islands are bustling with activity, and popular attractions, restaurants, and beaches may experience higher crowds. It's advisable to book accommodations and activities well in advance to secure your preferences during this busy period.

Shoulder Seasons (May to November):

The shoulder seasons, spanning from May to November, offer a different yet equally appealing experience for those seeking a more laid-back and budget-friendly trip. This period encompasses the Caribbean's hurricane season, but it's essential to note that major storms are relatively rare in Antigua and Barbuda.

During the shoulder seasons, temperatures remain warm, with occasional rain showers providing a refreshing break from the heat. The islands' landscapes transform into vibrant shades of green, creating a lush and picturesque backdrop. While humidity levels increase, the trade-off is fewer tourists, lower accommodation rates, and a quieter ambiance. Travelers with a penchant for serenity and a desire to explore the islands at a leisurely pace may find the shoulder seasons particularly appealing.

Consideration for Festivals and Events:

Beyond weather considerations, the timing of your visit can align with various festivals and events that add cultural richness to your experience. Antigua, in particular, is renowned for its Carnival celebrations held in late July and early August. This vibrant and lively event features colorful parades, lively music, and elaborate costumes, providing a unique insight into the local culture and traditions.

Sailing enthusiasts may want to plan their visit during Antigua Sailing Week, typically held in late April or early May. This international regatta attracts sailors and spectators alike, creating an electrifying atmosphere around English Harbour.

Making Your Decision:

Ultimately, choosing the best time to visit Antigua and Barbuda depends on your preferences, priorities, and the type of experience you seek. If you're drawn to the energy of peak season, with vibrant social scenes and an array of activities, then the dry months from December to April are ideal. On the other hand, if you prefer a more relaxed and budget-conscious trip, the shoulder seasons offer a quieter, greener, and more affordable alternative.

Before finalizing your travel dates, it's advisable to check the latest weather forecasts and monitor any travel advisories. Additionally, factor in the specific activities you wish to pursue, whether it's participating in lively events, enjoying water sports, or simply basking in the natural beauty of the islands. Armed with this knowledge, you can confidently choose the best time to visit Antigua and Barbuda and ensure a memorable and tailored Caribbean getaway.

1.3 Visa and Entry Requirements

One of the first steps in planning your journey to Antigua and Barbuda is understanding the visa and entry requirements. Navigating through these regulations ensures a smooth and stress-free arrival on the captivating islands.

Visa Requirements:

Antigua and Barbuda operate a visa policy that varies depending on your nationality. Fortunately, citizens from many countries, including the United States, Canada, the United Kingdom, and members of the European Union, do not require a visa for stays of up to 90 days. This lenient policy encourages tourism and simplifies the entry process for travelers from these nations.

The visa exemption period is typically sufficient for most tourists visiting Antigua and Barbuda for leisure purposes. However, it's crucial to check the most up-to-date information before your trip, as visa requirements and policies can change. The official government website or contacting the nearest embassy or consulate of Antigua and Barbuda in your home country are reliable sources for the latest updates.

Passport Requirements:

Regardless of your nationality, a valid passport is a non-negotiable requirement for entry into Antigua and Barbuda. Your passport must have at least six months of validity beyond your intended departure date from the islands. This ensures that you have ample time on your passport in case of any unexpected delays or changes to your travel plans.

It's advisable to make copies of your passport and store them separately from the original document. Additionally, having digital copies saved in a secure cloud-based storage service can be beneficial in case of loss or theft. These precautions will streamline the process of obtaining a replacement if needed.

Return or Onward Travel Ticket:

Upon arrival in Antigua and Barbuda, you may be required to present proof of return or onward travel. This requirement is in place to ensure that visitors do not overstay their allowed duration and have plans to leave the country within the stipulated timeframe.

Before departing for your journey, confirm your return ticket details and ensure that the dates align with the permitted duration of your stay. This confirmation can be in the form of a physical ticket or an electronic itinerary, but it must clearly indicate your departure date from Antigua and Barbuda.

Sufficient Funds for Stay:

To gain entry into Antigua and Barbuda, it's essential to demonstrate that you possess sufficient funds to cover the costs of your stay. This requirement aims to ensure that visitors have the financial means to support themselves during their time on the islands.

While the specific amount may not be explicitly defined, it is advisable to have access to funds that cover accommodation, meals, transportation, and any planned activities. This could be in the form of cash, traveler's checks, or credit cards. Having a combination of these options provides flexibility and ensures you are well-prepared for various situations.

Extension of Stay:

If, during your visit, you find yourself desiring an extension of your stay beyond the initially permitted duration, it's essential to be aware of the extension process. Extensions can typically be requested through the Antigua and Barbuda Immigration Department. However, it's crucial to initiate this process well in advance of your original departure date and be prepared to provide a valid reason for the extension.

Entry Requirements for Cruise Ship Passengers:

If you are arriving in Antigua and Barbuda via cruise ship, the entry requirements differ slightly. Cruise ship passengers are usually granted a stay of up to 24 hours without a visa. However, if you plan to stay longer or engage in activities beyond the port area, you must adhere to the standard visa and entry requirements outlined for other visitors.

Eastern Caribbean Dollar (XCD):

Antigua and Barbuda use the Eastern Caribbean Dollar (XCD) as their official currency. While U.S. dollars are widely accepted, it's recommended to familiarize yourself with the local currency and have a mix of cash and cards for convenience. Inform your bank of your travel dates to avoid any issues with card transactions, and consider exchanging a small amount of currency upon arrival for immediate expenses.

Pre-Travel Checklist:

In summary, here's a pre-travel checklist to ensure a seamless entry into Antigua and Barbuda:

- Valid Passport: Ensure your passport has at least six months of validity beyond your intended departure date.
- Visa Requirements: Check the visa requirements based on your nationality, and ensure you comply with the latest regulations.
- Return or Onward Travel Ticket: Confirm your return or onward travel details before departure.

- Sufficient Funds: Have access to funds that cover your stay, and be prepared to demonstrate financial capacity if required.
- Cruise Ship Entry: If arriving by cruise ship, understand the specific entry requirements and permitted stay duration.
- Currency: Familiarize yourself with the Eastern Caribbean Dollar and consider carrying a mix of cash and cards.
- Extension of Stay: If needed, be aware of the process for extending your stay and initiate it well in advance.

By adhering to these entry requirements and staying informed, you set the foundation for a worry-free and enjoyable experience in the enchanting islands of Antigua and Barbuda.

1.4 Budgeting and Money Matters

As you embark on planning your journey to the enchanting islands of Antigua and Barbuda, understanding the financial aspects of your trip is essential for a seamless and enjoyable experience. From accommodation and dining to activities and transportation, effective budgeting ensures you make the most of your time in this Caribbean paradise.

Creating a Realistic Budget:

Start your trip planning by creating a realistic budget that aligns with your travel preferences and financial capacity. Antigua and Barbuda offer a range of options, from luxury resorts to more budget-friendly guesthouses, allowing you to tailor your accommodations to your budget. Consider your daily expenses, including meals, activities, and transportation, and factor in any planned excursions or special experiences.

Accommodation Options:

Accommodation costs can vary widely in Antigua and Barbuda. The islands boast luxurious resorts with all-inclusive packages, charming boutique hotels, and more budget-friendly guesthouses. Determine the type of accommodation that suits your preferences and budget. Keep in mind that booking in advance can sometimes yield discounts or special offers, helping you maximize your budget.

Dining Choices and Costs:

Antigua and Barbuda offer a diverse culinary scene, featuring a mix of local and international cuisine. While dining at upscale restaurants can be a delightful experience, exploring local eateries and street food stalls can provide a more budget-friendly option. Consider a balance of both to savor the local flavors without overspending. Additionally, some accommodations may offer meal packages, providing a convenient and cost-effective dining solution.

Activities and Excursions:

Plan your activities and excursions based on your interests and budget constraints. Antigua and Barbuda offer an array of experiences, from water sports and boat tours to historical site visits and nature exploration. Research and prioritize the activities that align with your preferences, and inquire about package deals or group discounts to make the most of your budget.

Transportation Costs:

Factor in transportation costs when creating your budget. If you plan to rent a car, consider the associated fees, fuel costs, and parking expenses. Alternatively, public transportation and taxi services are available, providing convenient and cost-effective options for getting around the islands. Additionally, many accommodations offer shuttle services, so inquire about these options when booking your stay.

Currency and Payment Methods:

The official currency of Antigua and Barbuda is the Eastern Caribbean Dollar (XCD). However, U.S. dollars are widely accepted, and major credit cards are commonly used. Inform your bank of your travel dates to avoid any issues with card transactions. Having a mix of cash and cards is advisable, as some smaller establishments may prefer cash.

Special Considerations for All-Inclusive Resorts:

If you opt for an all-inclusive resort, carefully review the package details to understand what is included. While these packages may cover accommodation, meals, and some activities, certain services or premium experiences might incur additional charges. Clarify these details in advance to avoid unexpected expenses during your stay.

Shopping and Souvenirs:

While exploring the local markets and shops for souvenirs is a delightful part of any trip, it's essential to budget for these expenses. Handcrafted items, local art, and traditional souvenirs make for meaningful mementos of your Antigua and Barbuda adventure. Allocate a portion of your budget for shopping, and consider supporting local artisans and businesses.

Emergency Fund:

Always include an emergency fund in your budget for unforeseen circumstances or unplanned expenses. This reserve can be invaluable in situations like unexpected medical needs, changes in travel plans, or other emergencies. Having a financial buffer ensures you can navigate challenges without compromising the overall enjoyment of your trip.

Staying Informed about Departure Tax:

While there is no specific entry fee for tourists, Antigua and Barbuda have implemented a departure tax. This fee is often included in the cost of your airline ticket, but it's essential to confirm this with your airline. Departure taxes are subject to change, so staying informed about this aspect of your budget is advisable.

1.5 Essential Packing Tips

To ensure you're well-prepared for your Caribbean getaway, here are essential packing tips that will enhance your comfort and enjoyment during your stay.

1. Lightweight Clothing:

Antigua and Barbuda enjoy a warm tropical climate throughout the year, so pack lightweight, breathable clothing. Choose fabrics like cotton and linen that keep you cool in the heat. Loose-fitting dresses, shorts, and T-shirts are perfect for daytime explorations.

2. Swimwear and Beach Attire:

With numerous pristine beaches and crystal-clear waters, swimwear is a must-pack item. Whether you're lounging on the powdery sands or snorkeling in the vibrant coral reefs, having the right swim gear ensures you make the most of the islands' aquatic treasures.

3. Sun Protection Essentials:

The Caribbean sun can be intense, so packing sun protection essentials is crucial. Include a high SPF sunscreen, sunglasses with UV protection, and a wide-brimmed hat to shield yourself from the sun's rays. Reapply sunscreen regularly, especially if you're engaging in water activities.

4. Casual Evening Wear:

While the islands have a relaxed atmosphere, you might want to pack some casual evening wear for dinners at beachfront restaurants or sunset strolls. A light sundress or a collared shirt with comfortable trousers can strike the perfect balance between comfort and style.

5. Comfortable Footwear:

Given the laid-back vibe of Antigua and Barbuda, opt for comfortable footwear suitable for walking. Sandals, flip-flops, and breathable sneakers are ideal for exploring the islands' natural wonders and historic sites. If you plan on hiking, consider bringing sturdy, closed-toe shoes.

6. Rain Gear and Waterproof Accessories:

While the islands generally experience a dry season, there's always a chance of brief tropical showers. Pack a lightweight, compact rain jacket or poncho to stay dry. Consider bringing a waterproof case or bag for your electronics and important documents when engaging in water-based activities.

7. Insect Repellent:

Tropical destinations often come with their share of insects. Packing insect repellent is a wise precaution, especially if you plan on exploring nature reserves, hiking trails, or enjoying outdoor dining experiences. Opt for a DEET-based repellent for effective protection.

8. Portable Water Bottle:

Staying hydrated is essential in the Caribbean heat. Bring a reusable, portable water bottle to keep yourself refreshed throughout the day. You can refill it at your accommodation or carry it during your island explorations.

9. Snorkeling Gear:

If you're a fan of underwater adventures, consider packing your own snorkeling gear. While many tour operators provide equipment, having your own ensures a perfect fit and allows you to explore the marine wonders at your own pace.

10. Lightweight Backpack:

A lightweight and durable backpack is a valuable addition to your packing list. It's perfect for carrying essentials during day trips, beach outings, and hikes. Ensure it has enough compartments to organize your belongings efficiently.

11. Electrical Adapters and Chargers:

Antigua and Barbuda use the Eastern Caribbean Dollar and have standard North American electrical outlets. Bring the necessary electrical adapters and chargers for your devices to stay connected and capture memories of your island adventures.

12. Travel-Friendly Luggage Options:

Opt for travel-friendly luggage options that suit your needs. Durable, lightweight suitcases with ample storage space are ideal for longer stays, while a compact carry-on or backpack is convenient for shorter trips and day excursions.

1.5.1 Travel-friendly luggage options

The islands offer a diverse range of experiences, from exploring historical sites to enjoying water activities on pristine beaches. Having the appropriate luggage ensures you can navigate these experiences seamlessly while keeping your belongings secure and well-organized.

Considerations for Travel-friendly Luggage:

1. Durable and Lightweight Suitcases:

When choosing your primary suitcase, prioritize durability and weight. Opt for materials like polycarbonate or ballistic nylon that strike a balance between resilience and weight. The Caribbean climate can be warm, so having a lightweight suitcase makes it easier to manage, especially if you plan on moving between accommodations.

2. Spinner Wheels for Maneuverability:

Antigua and Barbuda's varied terrain, from beaches to urban areas, makes maneuverability essential. Choose a suitcase with spinner wheels for easy navigation through airports, hotel lobbies, and uneven surfaces. Spinner wheels provide 360-degree rotation, allowing you to glide effortlessly in any direction.

3. Expandable Design for Flexibility:

An expandable suitcase provides flexibility in packing, accommodating souvenirs or items acquired during your travels. This feature allows you to adjust the size of your luggage as needed, providing convenience without compromising on weight.

4. Built-in TSA-approved Locks:

Security is paramount, and having built-in TSA-approved locks adds an extra layer of protection. These locks allow airport security to inspect your luggage without damaging it. They offer peace of mind, especially if you plan to check in your suitcase during flights.

5. Carry-on Bag with Multiple Compartments:

For day trips and excursions, a well-organized carry-on bag is essential. Look for a bag with multiple compartments to keep your essentials easily accessible. Pockets for water bottles, sunscreen, and a camera ensure you're prepared for a day of exploration without the need to constantly rummage through your bag.

6. Comfortable Backpack for Day Adventures:

A comfortable backpack is invaluable for exploring Antigua and Barbuda's natural wonders. Choose one with padded shoulder straps and back support for optimal comfort, especially if you plan on hiking or walking for extended periods. Ensure it has enough space for essentials like water, snacks, and a camera.

Adapting Luggage to Activities:

1. Water-resistant Features:

Considering the islands' aquatic activities, having water-resistant features on your luggage is advantageous. This is especially relevant if you plan on spending time at the beach or participating in water sports. Water-resistant materials or built-in rain covers can protect your belongings from unexpected showers or splashes.

2. Versatile Daypack for Various Activities:

Antigua and Barbuda offer diverse experiences, from historical tours to beach outings. Having a versatile daypack that can transition seamlessly between these activities ensures you're well-prepared for anything. Look for a pack with adjustable straps and the ability to compress for easy storage.

3. Compact Folding Options for Flexibility:

If you anticipate bringing back more than you arrived with, consider compact folding options. Some luggage designs allow for easy compression or folding, making it practical for storage in your suitcase. This way, you can accommodate additional items without the need for extra baggage.

Practical Packing Tips:

1. Rolling vs. Folding Clothes:

To optimize space and minimize wrinkles, consider rolling your clothes instead of folding them. This packing technique not only saves space but also makes it easier to locate specific items in your suitcase.

2. Use Packing Cubes for Organization:

Packing cubes are a game-changer for staying organized during your trip. Categorize your clothes, accessories, and toiletries into separate cubes for easy access and a clutter-free suitcase.

3. Pack Essentials in Your Carry-on:

Important items such as medications, travel documents, and a change of clothes should be packed in your carry-on bag. This ensures you have essential items even if your checked luggage is delayed or misplaced.

CHAPTER TWO

GETTING ACQUAINTED WITH ANTIGUA AND BARBUDA

2.1 Overview of Antigua and Barbuda's Geography and Climate:

Nestled in the heart of the Caribbean, Antigua and Barbuda form a captivating pair of islands, each boasting a distinct character and charm. Geographically positioned in the Leeward Islands, Antigua, the larger of the two, enchants visitors with its rolling hills, sandy beaches, and a breathtaking coastline. In stark contrast, Barbuda, situated to the north of Antigua, exudes a serene ambiance, characterized by expansive pink sand beaches and a diverse array of ecosystems.

Antigua, often referred to as the "Land of 365 Beaches," lives up to its moniker with a collection of pristine shores, each presenting a unique blend of soft, white sand and crystalline turquoise waters. The island's topography is adorned with vibrant coral reefs, creating an underwater wonderland that beckons snorkelers and divers alike. The vibrant capital city, St. John's, stands as a bustling hub, seamlessly blending modern amenities with colonial charm. Meanwhile, the historic English Harbour proudly showcases a meticulously preserved naval dockyard, offering a glimpse into the island's maritime legacy.

In contrast, Barbuda unfolds as a tranquil haven, where expansive beaches, notably the world-renowned Pink Sand

Beach, invite solitude and relaxation. The island's interior unveils lush landscapes, teeming with diverse birdlife, including the largest frigate bird colony in the Western Hemisphere. The Codrington Lagoon and Frigate Bird Sanctuary stand as testament to Barbuda's unwavering commitment to preserving its natural heritage.

Antigua and Barbuda's climate epitomizes the tropical paradise archetype, boasting consistent warmth throughout the year. The dry season, extending from December to April, is tailor-made for sun-seekers and beach enthusiasts, providing idyllic conditions to bask in the Caribbean sun. Come the wet season, from May to November, refreshing yet brief showers breathe life into the landscapes, transforming the islands into lush, green paradises. Visitors can revel in the islands' beauty regardless of the season, with temperatures averaging between a balmy 75°F (24°C) and a delightful 87°F (31°C).

2.2 Historical and Cultural Background:

The rich tapestry of Antigua and Barbuda's history unfurls with influences from indigenous peoples, European colonizers, and the enduring legacy of African heritage. Long before the arrival of Europeans, the islands were home to the Arawak and Carib peoples, who left an indelible mark on the cultural landscape. In 1493, Christopher Columbus first sighted Antigua, but it was the British who laid the foundations for a lasting presence in the early 17th century.

The pivotal role of sugar cultivation became the linchpin of the islands' economy during the colonial era, propelling the demand for an extensive labor force. This demand led to the importation of African slaves, profoundly shaping the islands' demographics and contributing to the vibrant cultural mosaic witnessed today. The echoes of this colonial history reverberate through time, manifested in the well-preserved architecture of iconic sites such as Nelson's Dockyard, a testament to the naval legacy, and Betty's Hope, an evocative reminder of the sugar plantation era.

The year 1981 marked a transformative chapter in Antigua and Barbuda's history as the islands gained independence from British rule. This monumental event symbolized a newfound autonomy, allowing the islands to shape their destiny and celebrate their unique identity. Present-day Antigua and Barbuda revel in their cultural diversity, expressing it vibrantly through a myriad of festivals, most notably the exuberant Carnival. This lively celebration of Caribbean culture features colorful parades, infectious music, and traditional costumes, embodying the islands' spirit of resilience and unity.

The cultural vibrancy extends beyond festive celebrations to encompass the islands' art, music, and dance scenes. Calypso and reggae rhythms permeate the air, providing a sonic backdrop that mirrors the lively and dynamic spirit of the local populace. The artistic traditions, deeply rooted in the islands' history, are exemplified through local crafts such as pottery and basket weaving. These crafts offer a tangible link to the past, showcasing the creativity and skill that have been passed down through generations, ensuring the preservation of Antigua and Barbuda's rich cultural heritage. As visitors immerse themselves in the vibrant tapestry of this Caribbean duo, they become part of a living history, woven together by the threads of resilience, diversity, and the enduring spirit of Antigua and Barbuda.

2.3 Languages and Communication:

English stands as the official language of Antigua and Barbuda, a linguistic legacy that harks back to the islands' colonial past. This continuity simplifies communication for English-speaking visitors, eradicating language barriers commonly encountered in foreign travel. Navigating the vibrant streets of St. John's or engaging in business transactions becomes a seamless experience, as English serves as the primary means of communication.

Despite English being the dominant language, the islands also boast a rich linguistic tapestry with the widespread use of the local dialect, known as "Antiguan Creole" or "Bajan." While English prevails in official and business interactions, immersing oneself in the local dialect can significantly enhance the overall travel experience. Visitors often discover that incorporating a few basic phrases in Antiguan Creole, such as greetings and expressions of gratitude, elicits warm responses from the local community, fostering a deeper connection with the islanders.

In popular tourist areas and hospitality establishments, English remains the predominant language, ensuring clear communication for visitors. However, those seeking a more immersive cultural experience may venture into remote or traditional communities. Here, the opportunity to engage in the local dialect arises, providing a gateway to a more profound understanding of Antigua and Barbuda's cultural fabric. Conversations with locals in their native tongue unveil a richer narrative, offering insights into traditions, customs, and the islanders' way of life.

Beyond the spoken word, the islands' cultural communication extends into vibrant visual expressions. Colorful street art adorns the walls of towns, narrating stories of resilience and celebrating the dynamic heritage of Antigua and Barbuda. Traditional crafts showcase intricate designs that serve as a visual language, communicating the unique identity forged over centuries. From pottery to woven baskets, each piece of art carries the imprints of the islands' history, creating a visual symphony that resonates with the spirit of the Caribbean.

2.4 Currency Exchange Tips:

For tourists embarking on a journey to the idyllic islands of Antigua and Barbuda, understanding the nuances of currency exchange is crucial to ensuring a seamless and enjoyable travel experience. The official currency of Antigua and Barbuda is the Eastern Caribbean Dollar (XCD), denoted by the symbols "$" or "EC$." While the United States Dollar (USD) is widely accepted and sometimes even preferred, it's advisable for visitors to acquaint themselves with the local currency for smoother transactions and fair pricing.

Currency exchange services are readily available at various banks, authorized exchange offices, and some hotels throughout Antigua and Barbuda. To facilitate convenience, it's recommended to exchange a portion of your currency upon arrival. This ensures that you have Eastern Caribbean Dollars on hand, particularly useful when dealing with smaller establishments and vendors who may prefer local currency.

In major urban centers like St. John's, credit cards are widely accepted, providing an additional layer of financial flexibility for visitors. However, it's prudent to inform your bank of your travel plans beforehand to prevent any potential issues with card transactions.

ATMs are prevalent in urban areas, allowing tourists to withdraw Eastern Caribbean Dollars as needed. To avoid inconveniences, it's advisable to carry smaller denominations for day-to-day expenses, especially when exploring more remote areas where obtaining change may be limited.

While the United States Dollar is commonly accepted, visitors should be aware that some businesses may offer a fixed exchange rate, and others might calculate it based on daily rates. It's always helpful to inquire about the accepted form of payment in each establishment to avoid any misunderstandings.

Being mindful of the local currency dynamics not only facilitates financial transactions but also allows tourists to engage more authentically with the vibrant local culture. By embracing the use of Eastern Caribbean Dollars alongside the familiar United States Dollar, visitors can fully immerse themselves in the rich tapestry of experiences that Antigua and Barbuda have to offer, from bustling markets to charming local eateries.

CHAPTER THREE
MUST VISIT DESTINATIONS

3.1 Nelson's Dockyard:

Nestled on the southern shores of Antigua, Nelson's Dockyard stands as a testament to the island's rich maritime history and colonial legacy. This UNESCO World Heritage Site is a must-visit destination for tourists seeking a captivating blend of historical charm, architectural grandeur, and vibrant cultural experiences.

Historical Background:

Named after Admiral Horatio Nelson, the renowned British naval hero, Nelson's Dockyard dates back to the 18th century when it served as a strategic naval base for the British Royal Navy during the height of the Caribbean's colonial era. The dockyard played a crucial role as a repair and maintenance facility for ships traversing the Atlantic, safeguarding British interests in the Caribbean.

Architectural Marvels:

Visitors to Nelson's Dockyard are greeted by a captivating ensemble of colonial-era buildings, cobblestone streets, and meticulously preserved naval structures. The imposing Copper and Lumber Store, once a warehouse for ship supplies, now houses shops and galleries, showcasing local art and crafts. The Admiral's Inn, with its timeless elegance, offers a glimpse into the luxury of the colonial era and provides a splendid setting for dining with a view of the harbor.

The heart of the dockyard is undoubtedly the Georgian-era Naval Officer's House, a magnificent structure that has been meticulously restored to its former glory. The Dockyard Museum, located within the Officer's House, provides an in-depth exploration of the site's history, featuring artifacts, exhibits, and interactive displays that bring the past to life.

Must-See Attractions:

- Dockyard Museum: Delve into the rich maritime history of Antigua at the Dockyard Museum. Exhibits showcase the evolution of Nelson's Dockyard, the significance of the harbor, and the cultural tapestry of the island.
- Admiral's Inn: Enjoy a delightful culinary experience at the Admiral's Inn, where local and international cuisine is served against a backdrop of colonial charm. The terrace provides breathtaking views of the harbor and the yachts anchored in the marina.
- Copper and Lumber Store: Explore this historic building, now transformed into a shopping haven. From local crafts to unique souvenirs, the store offers a curated selection that reflects the spirit of Antigua.
- Naval Officer's House: Wander through the elegant halls of the Georgian-era Naval Officer's House, appreciating the architectural finesse and gaining insights into the lives of the officers who once resided here.
- Lookout Points: Climb to the Shirley Heights Lookout for panoramic views of English Harbour and the

surrounding landscapes. This vantage point provides a stunning perspective of the dockyard and its natural surroundings.

Cultural Experiences:

Beyond its historical significance, Nelson's Dockyard is a vibrant cultural hub that hosts various events and activities throughout the year. From art exhibitions and regattas to music festivals, the dockyard pulsates with energy, offering tourists an opportunity to engage with the local community and immerse themselves in the island's dynamic culture.

Regattas and Sailing Events:

Antigua is renowned for its sailing culture, and Nelson's Dockyard is at the epicenter of this maritime passion. The annual Antigua Sailing Week, a world-class regatta, attracts sailing enthusiasts from around the globe. Visitors can witness the spectacle of sleek yachts competing against the backdrop of the historic dockyard, creating a visual feast for both seasoned sailors and casual observers.

Guided Tours and Workshops:

To enhance the visitor experience, guided tours are available, providing detailed insights into the dockyard's history, architecture, and cultural significance. Knowledgeable guides share anecdotes, historical facts, and intriguing stories that breathe life into the weathered bricks and cobbled streets.

For those seeking a hands-on experience, workshops and interactive sessions are offered, allowing tourists to try their hand at traditional shipbuilding techniques or indulge in artistic endeavors inspired by the island's vibrant culture.

Practical Tips for Visitors:

1. Operating Hours: Nelson's Dockyard is typically open from morning until late afternoon. It's advisable to check the specific operating hours on the official website or inquire locally before planning your visit.

2. Entrance Fees: While there might be nominal fees for certain attractions within the dockyard, the experience of strolling through the grounds and enjoying the architectural wonders is often free of charge.

3. Photography: The dockyard offers endless photo opportunities. Ensure your camera or smartphone is fully charged to capture the historical ambiance, scenic views, and vibrant events.

4. Footwear: Wear comfortable walking shoes, as exploring the dockyard involves traversing cobblestone streets and uneven surfaces.

5. Local Events Calendar: Check the local events calendar before planning your visit. Timing your trip to coincide with regattas, festivals, or cultural events can provide an enriched experience.

3.2 Shirley Heights:

For tourists embarking on an exploration of Antigua and Barbuda, one destination that stands out prominently on the must-visit list is the iconic Shirley Heights. Renowned for its breathtaking panoramic views, historical significance, and vibrant atmosphere, Shirley Heights is an essential stop for those seeking a comprehensive and enriching Caribbean experience.

Overview of Shirley Heights:

Perched atop the lush hills overlooking English Harbour on the southern tip of Antigua, Shirley Heights provides visitors with a mesmerizing vantage point that encompasses not only the harbor but also the expansive azure waters of the Caribbean Sea. This elevated vantage point has earned Shirley Heights its reputation as one of the best viewpoints in the entire Caribbean, making it an absolute must-visit for any traveler seeking unparalleled scenic beauty.

Historical Significance:

Shirley Heights has a rich historical background dating back to the 18th century. Originally a military complex built by the British to protect the valuable naval base in English Harbour, the site was named after Sir Thomas Shirley, the Governor of the Leeward Islands during that period. The strategic importance of Shirley Heights during the colonial era is evident in the well-preserved remnants of military structures that dot the area, including barracks, gunpowder magazines, and defensive walls.

Exploring the historical elements of Shirley Heights provides visitors with a tangible connection to the island's past. The remnants of the military structures offer a glimpse into the challenges faced by the colonial powers as they sought to defend their interests in the Caribbean. Interpretive signs and guided tours are available to provide deeper insights into the historical context of Shirley Heights.

Panoramic Views and Sunsets:

The primary allure of Shirley Heights lies in its unparalleled panoramic views, making it an ideal spot to witness the breathtaking beauty of Antigua. Visitors can enjoy sweeping vistas of English Harbour, Falmouth Harbour, and the lush coastline that extends towards the horizon. The panoramic views are particularly captivating during the golden hours of sunrise and sunset, creating a visual spectacle that captivates the senses.

Sunday evenings at Shirley Heights are renowned for the famous Shirley Heights Sunset Party. Locals and tourists alike gather to soak in the magical ambiance as the sun dips below the Caribbean Sea, casting a warm glow over the landscape. Live music, local bands, and the enticing aroma of Caribbean cuisine create an unforgettable atmosphere, making the Sunset Party a quintessential Caribbean experience.

Hiking Trails and Nature Walks:

Aside from its historical and visual appeal, Shirley Heights offers hiking enthusiasts a network of scenic trails and nature walks that wind through the surrounding hills. Exploring these trails allows visitors to connect with the natural beauty of Antigua, encountering indigenous flora and fauna along the way. The moderate hiking difficulty ensures that both casual strollers and avid hikers can enjoy the exploration.

One of the popular trails leads to the top of Shirley Heights, offering an invigorating hike with rewarding views at the summit. The surrounding landscape, adorned with cacti, shrubs, and occasional glimpses of wildlife, provides a serene escape into the island's interior.

Shirley's Fort:

As visitors ascend Shirley Heights, they encounter Shirley's Fort, an integral part of the historical complex. The fortifications, constructed with locally sourced stone, showcase the architectural prowess of the colonial era. Exploring the fort allows tourists to step back in time, imagining the strategic importance of this location in safeguarding the island against potential threats.

Shirley's Fort, with its commanding position overlooking the coastline, provides a glimpse into the challenges faced by the British forces defending the island. The well-preserved cannons and defensive structures evoke a sense of the military history that unfolded in this very location.

Nelson's Dockyard:

Connected by a scenic coastal trail, Shirley Heights is in close proximity to Nelson's Dockyard, a UNESCO World Heritage Site. Visitors can extend their exploration from Shirley Heights to this historic naval dockyard, providing a comprehensive understanding of Antigua's maritime heritage.

Nelson's Dockyard, named after Admiral Horatio Nelson, is a meticulously preserved 18th-century dockyard that served as a strategic hub for the British Navy in the Caribbean. The site includes historic buildings, museums, and a marina, offering a deep dive into the island's naval history.

3.3 Stingray City:

Nestled along the shores of Antigua, Stingray City stands as a remarkable testament to the captivating beauty of the Caribbean's underwater world. For tourists seeking an unforgettable aquatic experience, this marine haven offers a unique encounter with the graceful and friendly Southern Stingrays.

Location and Access:

Stingray City is situated in the North Sound of Antigua, a pristine marine environment surrounded by coral reefs and clear turquoise waters. Accessible by boat, the journey to Stingray City typically starts from popular hubs like Dickenson Bay or Jolly Harbour. Numerous tour operators offer excursions to this renowned site, providing visitors with both transportation and expert guidance.

Encounter with Southern Stingrays:

Upon arriving at Stingray City, visitors are greeted by the mesmerizing sight of crystal-clear waters teeming with Southern Stingrays. Known for their docile nature, these marine creatures have made Stingray City their home, creating a unique opportunity for tourists to interact with them in their natural environment.

Guided tours facilitate safe and educational encounters with the stingrays, allowing visitors to wade or snorkel in the shallow, sandy-bottomed areas where the rays congregate. The guides, well-versed in the behavior and ecology of stingrays, provide insightful commentary, enhancing the overall experience.

Snorkeling and Underwater Exploration:

Stingray City not only offers the chance to interact with stingrays but also provides a splendid snorkeling experience. The surrounding coral reefs harbor a diverse array of marine life, including colorful tropical fish and vibrant coral formations. Snorkelers can explore this underwater wonderland, discovering the beauty and biodiversity that thrives beneath the surface.

Stingray City: Dos and Don'ts:

To ensure a safe and enjoyable experience at Stingray City, it's essential for tourists to adhere to some basic guidelines:

- Respect the Stingrays: While Southern Stingrays are generally gentle, it's crucial to approach them with respect and follow the instructions of the guides. Avoid sudden movements and refrain from touching their tails, as this is the most sensitive part of their bodies.
- Listen to the Guides: The knowledgeable guides play a crucial role in ensuring a positive experience for both visitors and stingrays. Pay attention to their instructions on how to interact with the rays and navigate the underwater environment.
- Use Reef-Friendly Sunscreen: When preparing for a visit to Stingray City, it's advisable to use reef-friendly sunscreen to protect both your skin and the delicate marine ecosystem.

Educational Component:

Stingray City is not only a place for thrilling encounters but also an opportunity for education. Guides often share fascinating insights into the behavior, biology, and ecological significance of Southern Stingrays. Visitors gain a deeper understanding of these magnificent creatures and their vital role in maintaining the balance of the marine ecosystem.

Photography and Memories:

The stunning backdrop of Stingray City provides an ideal setting for capturing memorable moments. Snorkelers and waders can document their interactions with the stingrays, creating lasting memories of this extraordinary experience. Many tour operators also offer underwater photography services, allowing visitors to take home professionally captured images of their aquatic adventure.

Stingray City in Barbuda:

While Antigua boasts its own Stingray City, Barbuda offers a unique version of this attraction. The Pink Sand Beach in Barbuda is known for its powdery pink sands and crystal-clear waters, and it's not uncommon to encounter friendly rays in the shallows. This provides an additional opportunity for tourists exploring both islands to experience the magic of Stingray City in different settings.

Combining Stingray City with Other Excursions:

Stingray City is often part of larger excursions that include additional attractions. Visitors can opt for combo tours that may include snorkeling at nearby coral reefs, exploring hidden coves, or even a visit to a secluded beach. Combining Stingray City with other activities allows tourists to make the most of their time on the water and explore the diverse offerings of Antigua and Barbuda.

Planning Your Stingray City Adventure:

When planning a visit to Stingray City, it's advisable to consider the following:

- Tour Operator Selection: Choose a reputable and licensed tour operator with experienced guides who prioritize both safety and environmental conservation.
- Tour Duration: Stingray City excursions typically last a few hours, so plan accordingly and allocate sufficient time to fully enjoy the experience.
- What to Bring: Pack essentials such as swimwear, sunscreen, a hat, and a waterproof camera to capture the highlights of your Stingray City adventure.
- Booking in Advance: As Stingray City is a popular attraction, especially during peak tourist seasons, it's advisable to book your excursion in advance to secure your spot.

3.4 Codrington Lagoon and Frigate Bird Sanctuary (Barbuda):

This ecological marvel beckons tourists to embark on an immersive journey into the heart of Barbuda's diverse ecosystems, providing a unique and unforgettable experience.

Location and Accessibility:

Situated on the western side of Barbuda, the Codrington Lagoon and Frigate Bird Sanctuary are easily accessible from the island's main settlement, Codrington. Tourists can reach Codrington by various means, including boat charters, organized tours, or private rentals. The sanctuary is a haven for nature enthusiasts, offering an opportunity to explore the pristine lagoon and witness the majestic frigate birds in their natural habitat.

Frigate Birds:

The Frigate Bird Sanctuary is renowned for hosting the largest frigate bird colony in the Western Hemisphere, making it a must-visit destination for birdwatchers and wildlife enthusiasts. The sanctuary provides a sanctuary for these captivating birds, allowing visitors to observe their nesting, mating rituals, and graceful flight patterns. The most prominent species is the Magnificent Frigatebird, distinguished by its striking black plumage and long, angular wings.

Unique Ecosystems:

The Codrington Lagoon itself is a mesmerizing expanse of shallow, brackish water surrounded by mangroves, creating a vital ecosystem for numerous bird species and marine life. The mangroves serve as a nursery for fish, contributing to the overall biodiversity of the area. Visitors can explore the lagoon on guided boat tours, offering a peaceful and informative journey through the sanctuary's interconnected waterways.

Seasonal Highlights:

The best time to visit the Codrington Lagoon and Frigate Bird Sanctuary is during the breeding season, which typically occurs from September to April. During this period, the air is filled with the distinct sounds of frigate birds, and the skies become a captivating display of their aerial acrobatics. Witnessing male frigate birds inflating their bright red throat pouches to attract mates is a spectacle that adds to the allure of this natural sanctuary.

Guided Tours and Responsible Tourism:

To fully appreciate the sanctuary's ecological significance, guided tours are highly recommended. Knowledgeable local guides provide insights into the delicate balance of the ecosystem, the migratory patterns of the birds, and the conservation efforts in place. Responsible tourism practices, such as maintaining a respectful distance from nesting sites and adhering to designated paths, contribute to the preservation of this natural haven.

Conservation Efforts:

The Codrington Lagoon and Frigate Bird Sanctuary are integral to Barbuda's commitment to environmental conservation. Efforts have been made to protect and sustain these critical ecosystems, ensuring the continued survival of the frigate bird population and the overall biodiversity of the lagoon. Visitors are encouraged to support these conservation initiatives and gain a deeper understanding of the delicate interplay between human activities and the natural world.

Barbuda's Unique Appeal:

Exploring the Codrington Lagoon and Frigate Bird Sanctuary is not just a wildlife adventure; it's an opportunity to delve into the unique charm of Barbuda. The island's tranquility, combined with its untouched natural beauty, creates an atmosphere of serenity that captivates every visitor. As part of a broader exploration of Barbuda's offerings, the sanctuary adds a touch of ecological wonder to the tapestry of experiences on this Caribbean gem.

3.5 Devil's Bridge:

Devil's Bridge, a captivating natural wonder situated on the eastern coast of Antigua, stands as a must-visit destination for tourists seeking both breathtaking landscapes and a touch of the island's rich geological history. This remarkable limestone arch formation has become an iconic symbol of Antigua, drawing visitors with its dramatic beauty and compelling tales.

Geological Marvel and Formation:

Devil's Bridge is a testament to the powerful forces of nature, shaped by the relentless action of the Atlantic Ocean against the rugged limestone coastline. Over the centuries, the ceaseless waves have carved out a natural arch, creating a striking bridge that spans across the turbulent waters. The bridge earned its intriguing name from the perilous conditions it presents, with the tumultuous waves crashing against the rocky cliffs, creating an awe-inspiring spectacle.

Location and Accessibility:

The bridge is conveniently located on the eastern side of Antigua, easily accessible by road. A scenic drive through the island's interior or along the coastline brings visitors to this natural wonder. The journey itself provides glimpses of Antigua's diverse landscapes, from lush greenery to the expansive blue hues of the Atlantic.

Panoramic Views and Coastal Beauty:

Upon arrival at Devil's Bridge, visitors are greeted with panoramic views of the rugged coastline and the vast Atlantic Ocean. The bridge offers an ideal vantage point to witness the powerful waves crashing against the cliffs, creating a mesmerizing display of nature's forces. The contrast between the azure waters, the rugged rock formations, and the surrounding greenery adds to the allure of the site.

Historical and Cultural Significance:

Beyond its geological marvel, Devil's Bridge holds historical and cultural significance for the people of Antigua. The site serves as a poignant reminder of the island's dark past, as it is believed that enslaved Africans, brought to Antigua to work on the sugar plantations, would escape to this desolate location, choosing to end their lives rather than endure the harsh conditions of slavery. As such, Devil's Bridge is a place of reflection, allowing visitors to connect with the island's history and pay homage to those who suffered during this period.

Caution and Safety:

While Devil's Bridge offers an awe-inspiring experience, it's important for visitors to exercise caution. The powerful waves and rocky terrain can be hazardous, and venturing too close to the edges can pose risks. It's advisable to stay within designated viewing areas, especially during periods of rough seas. Respect for the natural environment and adherence to safety guidelines contribute to a positive and responsible visitor experience.

Photography Opportunities:

Photographers and nature enthusiasts will find Devil's Bridge to be a treasure trove of visual delights. The changing moods of the ocean, the striking contrast between the rugged cliffs and the sea, and the natural framing provided by the arch make it a prime location for capturing memorable moments. Sunrise and sunset visits are particularly popular, offering a magical play of light and shadows.

Nearby Attractions:

Devil's Bridge is not isolated in its allure; the surrounding area offers additional attractions for those exploring the eastern side of Antigua. Long Bay, known for its pristine stretch of sandy beach, is nearby and provides a tranquil setting for relaxation and water activities. Bird enthusiasts can venture to Indian Town Point, a nearby area known for its birdwatching opportunities and scenic landscapes.

Cultural Immersion and Guided Tours:

To enhance the experience, guided tours are available, providing insights into the geological processes shaping Devil's Bridge and the cultural significance it holds. Local guides share stories passed down through generations, adding depth to the visitor's understanding of this natural wonder.

Accessibility for All:

Devil's Bridge is accessible to visitors of all ages and physical abilities. The site has designated viewing areas that cater to different preferences, whether one prefers to admire the scenery from a distance or get closer to feel the power of the crashing waves. The accessibility of Devil's Bridge makes it an inclusive destination for families, nature lovers, and those with varying mobility levels.

Visitor Tips:

1. Timing: Consider visiting Devil's Bridge during low tide for a safer and more enjoyable experience. However, be aware that the waves can be more intense during periods of rough seas.

2. Footwear: Wear sturdy footwear with good grip, especially if exploring the rocky areas around Devil's Bridge. The terrain can be uneven, and comfortable shoes ensure a secure footing.

3. Sun Protection: Antigua's sun can be intense, so wear sunscreen, a hat, and sunglasses to protect yourself from the

sun's rays, especially if visiting during the peak daylight hours.

4. Respect Nature: While exploring Devil's Bridge, respect the natural surroundings. Avoid littering, and refrain from touching or disturbing the local flora and fauna.

5. Guided Tours: Consider joining a guided tour to gain a deeper understanding of the geological processes and cultural significance of Devil's Bridge. Local guides offer valuable insights that enhance the overall experience.

3.6 Half Moon Bay:

Nestled along the eastern coast of Antigua, Half Moon Bay stands as a testament to the pristine beauty that defines the landscapes of Antigua and Barbuda. Renowned for its breathtaking views, powdery white sands, and crystal-clear turquoise waters, Half Moon Bay is a must-visit destination for travelers seeking a tranquil oasis away from the bustling tourist hotspots.

Location and Accessibility:

Half Moon Bay is situated approximately 10 miles southeast of St. John's, the capital city of Antigua. While the journey to this idyllic destination involves navigating some winding roads, the mesmerizing scenery along the way sets the stage for the paradise that awaits. Visitors can opt for various transportation options, including rental cars, guided tours, or even local buses, to reach this hidden gem.

The Beach Experience:

As one approaches Half Moon Bay, the first glimpse of its crescent-shaped shoreline framed by lush greenery is nothing short of enchanting. The beach, stretching over a mile, boasts fine, powdery white sand that feels like silk beneath your feet. The gentle curve of the bay creates a natural amphitheater, providing a sense of seclusion and privacy, making it an ideal spot for a tranquil escape.

The clear, shallow waters of Half Moon Bay invite visitors to indulge in a refreshing swim or simply wade along the shoreline. The gradual slope of the ocean floor makes it a safe and family-friendly environment for swimmers of all ages. Snorkeling enthusiasts will find the bay's coral reefs teeming with marine life, offering a glimpse into the vibrant underwater world of Antigua.

Breathtaking Scenery:

Beyond its inviting waters, Half Moon Bay treats visitors to breathtaking panoramic views. The rolling hills surrounding the bay create a dramatic backdrop, enhancing the sense of tranquility and natural beauty. Whether it's capturing the sunrise casting a warm glow over the bay or witnessing the sunset painting the sky in hues of pink and orange, the scenery at Half Moon Bay is a photographer's delight.

Secluded Serenity:

One of the most appealing aspects of Half Moon Bay is its relatively secluded nature. While Antigua and Barbuda are known for their popular tourist destinations, Half Moon Bay offers a more serene and laid-back atmosphere. The limited development in the area preserves the bay's natural charm, allowing visitors to unwind in a peaceful setting surrounded by the sounds of gentle waves and rustling palm trees.

Picnic Paradise:

For those who prefer a more intimate experience, Half Moon Bay provides the perfect setting for a beachside picnic. Shaded areas along the beach offer respite from the sun, allowing visitors to relax and enjoy a leisurely meal while taking in the stunning ocean views. Local vendors occasionally set up shop, offering refreshing coconut water or handmade crafts, adding to the authentic Caribbean experience.

Local Flavors:

Exploring the surroundings of Half Moon Bay can lead to delightful encounters with local flavors. Visitors may chance upon small, charming beach bars or food stalls where they can savor traditional Caribbean dishes and freshly caught seafood. Engaging with locals in these settings often provides a glimpse into the warm hospitality and vibrant culture of Antigua and Barbuda.

Practical Tips:

To make the most of a visit to Half Moon Bay, travelers should consider a few practical tips. Bringing essentials like sunscreen, hats, and ample water is crucial to staying comfortable under the Caribbean sun. Snorkeling gear is also recommended for those eager to explore the underwater wonders. It's advisable to check weather conditions before planning a visit, as the bay may experience stronger waves during certain times of the year.

While Half Moon Bay offers a serene retreat, it's essential to be mindful of leaving no trace. Responsible tourism practices, such as proper disposal of waste, contribute to preserving the natural beauty of this coastal haven for future generations.

3.7 Betty's Hope:

One must-visit destination that encapsulates the islands' intriguing past is Betty's Hope, a historic sugar plantation situated on the island of Antigua. Exploring Betty's Hope offers a captivating journey into the heart of the islands' colonial history, providing visitors with a nuanced understanding of Antigua and Barbuda's cultural evolution.

Historical Roots:

Betty's Hope, established in the 17th century, stands as one of the earliest sugar plantations in Antigua. Named after the daughter of Christopher Codrington, the plantation was a significant player in the sugar industry during the height of colonial rule. The Codrington family, instrumental in shaping the economic landscape of Antigua, operated Betty's Hope as a profitable enterprise, relying heavily on enslaved labor for sugar cultivation and processing.

The Sugar Mill and Factory:

A central feature of Betty's Hope is its well-preserved sugar mill and factory, offering a glimpse into the labor-intensive process of turning sugarcane into crystallized sweetness. The towering stone windmill, an iconic symbol of the plantation, serves as a silent witness to centuries of toil and industry. Guided tours take visitors through the various stages of sugar production, providing insights into the machinery, boiling houses, and the intricate process that once fueled the Caribbean's sugar economy.

Museum and Interpretation Center:

To further enrich the visitor experience, Betty's Hope boasts a museum and interpretation center. Here, artifacts, documents, and exhibits narrate the plantation's history, shedding light on the lives of both the plantation owners and the enslaved individuals who contributed to its prosperity. The museum offers a thought-provoking exploration of the complex social dynamics and economic forces that shaped Betty's Hope and, by extension, the broader history of Antigua.

Surrounding Landscape and Nature Trails:

Beyond its historical significance, Betty's Hope is nestled within a scenic landscape that invites exploration. Nature trails wind through the plantation, allowing visitors to appreciate the lush surroundings and providing opportunities for birdwatching. The juxtaposition of the natural beauty against the remnants of the plantation creates a serene atmosphere, inviting reflection on the intersection of human history and the Caribbean's breathtaking ecosystems.

Cultural Events and Festivals:

Betty's Hope comes alive during cultural events and festivals that celebrate Antigua and Barbuda's heritage. Special programs and activities are often organized at the plantation, providing visitors with an immersive experience. Traditional music, dance, and culinary delights add vibrancy to the historical setting, creating a dynamic fusion of past and present.

Community Engagement:

Betty's Hope is not just a historical site; it is an integral part of the local community. Engaging with residents and local guides during visits can offer a more personalized perspective on the significance of Betty's Hope. Conversations with those passionate about preserving the island's heritage can provide visitors with unique insights and anecdotes, fostering a deeper connection to the Antiguan way of life.

3.8 Antigua Rainforest Canopy Tour:

For the adventure-seeking tourist, the Antigua Rainforest Canopy Tour stands out as a thrilling and immersive experience that provides a unique perspective of the islands' lush and diverse ecosystems.

Overview of the Antigua Rainforest Canopy Tour:

The Antigua Rainforest Canopy Tour is an exhilarating adventure that allows visitors to soar above the rainforest canopy, immersing themselves in the natural beauty and biodiversity that the islands have to offer. This eco-friendly excursion combines the thrill of ziplining with an educational journey through the rich flora and fauna of Antigua's rainforest.

Location and Accessibility:

The tour is conveniently located near the Fig Tree Drive, a scenic route winding through Antigua's interior. Easily accessible from popular tourist areas, this adventure is within reach for visitors staying in St. John's or any of the coastal resorts. The tour operators typically provide transportation, making it a hassle-free experience for tourists looking to explore beyond the beaches.

The Ziplining Experience:

The highlight of the Antigua Rainforest Canopy Tour is undoubtedly the ziplining experience. Visitors are securely harnessed and guided through a series of platforms, suspended bridges, and ziplines that traverse the treetops. The course offers a range of ziplines, catering to both beginners and thrill-seekers, with varying lengths and heights above the forest floor.

As participants glide through the air, they are treated to breathtaking panoramic views of the rainforest, providing a bird's-eye perspective of the diverse vegetation and vibrant wildlife. The ziplines are strategically positioned to offer glimpses of hidden waterfalls, dense foliage, and the chirping birds that call the rainforest home.

Educational Nature Walks:

Beyond the adrenaline-pumping ziplining, the tour includes guided nature walks along well-maintained trails. Knowledgeable guides lead participants through the rainforest, sharing insights into the unique plant species, medicinal herbs, and the ecological importance of preserving this delicate ecosystem.

Tourists have the opportunity to learn about the diverse bird species inhabiting the rainforest, including the colorful and elusive native parrots. The guides' expertise extends to identifying various tree species, explaining their roles in maintaining the ecological balance, and highlighting the importance of sustainable tourism practices.

Eco-Friendly Practices:

The Antigua Rainforest Canopy Tour places a strong emphasis on eco-friendly and sustainable tourism. The construction of the zipline course is designed to minimize environmental impact, with platforms strategically placed to avoid disruption to the natural habitat. Guides educate visitors on the importance of conservation and responsible tourism, encouraging a deeper appreciation for the delicate balance of the rainforest ecosystem.

Booking and Logistics:

Booking the Antigua Rainforest Canopy Tour is a straightforward process, with various tour operators offering packages that include transportation, equipment rental, and expert guides. It's advisable to make reservations in advance, especially during peak tourist seasons, to secure a spot on this popular adventure.

Participants are typically required to wear closed-toe shoes and comfortable clothing suitable for outdoor activities. The tour operators provide all necessary safety equipment, including harnesses and helmets, ensuring a secure and enjoyable experience for visitors of all ages.

Ideal Times to Experience the Canopy Tour:

The Antigua Rainforest Canopy Tour is available year-round, offering a unique experience regardless of the season. However, participants may want to consider weather conditions for the best overall experience. The dry season, from December to April, provides clear skies and comfortable temperatures, enhancing the visibility of the rainforest's beauty. The wet season, from May to November, introduces a lush, green landscape but may include brief rain showers.

Combining Adventure with Relaxation:

For tourists seeking a well-rounded Antiguan experience, combining the Rainforest Canopy Tour with other activities and attractions is highly recommended. After the adrenaline rush of ziplining, visitors can unwind on the pristine beaches, explore historic sites like Nelson's Dockyard, or indulge in the local culinary scene in St. John's.

Safety Measures and Considerations:

The Antigua Rainforest Canopy Tour prioritizes safety, and participants undergo a comprehensive briefing before embarking on the adventure. Guides ensure that all safety harnesses and equipment are properly fitted, and participants are encouraged to follow guidelines for a secure and enjoyable experience. Pregnant women, individuals with heart conditions, or those with mobility issues may be advised against participating in the ziplining component of the tour.

3.9 Fig Tree Drive:

This scenic drive, stretching approximately 12 miles, winds its way through the island's interior, providing visitors with a unique perspective of Antigua's natural beauty and cultural richness.

Starting Point:

Fig Tree Drive begins in the verdant hills near the village of John Hughes on the island's southwest coast. As you embark on this scenic adventure, the drive unfolds like a carefully crafted tapestry, revealing the diverse facets of Antigua's topography and heritage.

Lush Landscapes and Agricultural Bounty:

As you traverse Fig Tree Drive, you'll be greeted by a kaleidoscope of greenery and vibrant vegetation. The drive takes you through rolling hills adorned with flourishing banana and citrus plantations, showcasing Antigua's agricultural bounty. The lush landscapes provide a soothing backdrop, creating an immersive experience for nature enthusiasts and photographers alike.

Farming Villages and Local Charm:

Fig Tree Drive meanders through several charming villages, offering tourists a glimpse into the daily lives of the island's residents. Villages such as Bethesda and Liberta are known for their warm hospitality and local charm. Take the opportunity to interact with the friendly locals, sample traditional snacks, and perhaps purchase handmade crafts as souvenirs, adding an authentic touch to your Antiguan experience.

Historical Points of Interest:

En route, Fig Tree Drive passes by historical points of interest that provide insights into Antigua's colonial past. Old estates, remnants of sugar mills, and other historical landmarks dot the landscape, serving as tangible reminders of the island's history. A stop at places like Betty's Hope, one of Antigua's oldest sugar plantations, allows you to delve into the island's economic foundations and its journey through time.

Photographic Opportunities:

For photography enthusiasts, Fig Tree Drive is a treasure trove of captivating scenes. The ever-changing vistas, from hillside panoramas to glimpses of the Caribbean Sea in the distance, offer numerous opportunities to capture the essence of Antigua. Be sure to have your camera ready to immortalize the scenic beauty that unfolds with every twist and turn.

Flora and Fauna:

Nature lovers will appreciate the drive's proximity to Antigua's rich biodiversity. The route takes you through lush rainforest areas, providing a chance to spot diverse flora and fauna. Keep an eye out for indigenous bird species, vibrant butterflies, and the occasional glimpse of the island's wildlife. Birdwatchers will particularly enjoy the varied avian population that inhabits the surrounding forests.

Countryside Retreats:

Fig Tree Drive also introduces visitors to the concept of countryside retreats and eco-friendly accommodations. Nestled amidst the rolling hills, these retreats offer a peaceful escape from the bustling coastal areas. Consider extending your stay at one of these serene establishments to fully immerse yourself in the tranquility of Antigua's countryside.

Local Cuisine and Refreshments:

Exploring Fig Tree Drive is not just a visual feast but also a culinary adventure. Along the route, you'll encounter local eateries and roadside stalls offering authentic Antiguan cuisine. Sample traditional dishes such as fungi and pepper pot, savoring the flavors of the island. The drive provides an excellent opportunity to indulge in local gastronomy while taking in the breathtaking surroundings.

Artistic Expressions Along the Drive:

As you wind your way through Fig Tree Drive, you'll encounter artistic expressions that add to the cultural tapestry of Antigua. From vibrant murals depicting local life to sculptures celebrating the island's heritage, these artistic touches contribute to the drive's unique character. Take the time to appreciate the creativity that dots the landscape, underscoring Antigua's commitment to the arts.

Guided Tours and Self-Exploration:

While some visitors may choose to embark on a self-guided exploration of Fig Tree Drive, guided tours are also available.

Knowledgeable local guides can offer deeper insights into the history, ecology, and cultural significance of the areas traversed. Whether self-exploring or joining a guided tour, the drive allows you to set your own pace and absorb the beauty at every turn.

Best Times to Experience Fig Tree Drive:

While Fig Tree Drive is enchanting year-round, the best times to experience its full splendor may be during the dry season, from December to April. The clear skies and mild temperatures enhance the scenic beauty and make for comfortable exploration. However, the wet season, from May to November, brings a different allure, with the landscape bathed in lush greenery and occasional refreshing showers.

3.10 Valley Church Beach:

This pristine stretch of shoreline is a must-visit destination for tourists seeking tranquility, crystal-clear waters, and the quintessential tropical beach experience.

Location and Access:

Valley Church Beach is conveniently situated near Jolly Harbour, a popular resort area on the western side of Antigua. Accessing this tropical haven is relatively straightforward, whether by rental car, taxi, or organized tours. A short drive from St. John's, the capital city, brings visitors to the doorstep of this serene oasis.

Natural Beauty:

Upon arrival, visitors are greeted by the breathtaking panorama of Valley Church Beach. The powdery white sand, framed by swaying palm trees, creates a postcard-perfect setting. The beach stretches along a gentle curve, inviting guests to explore its full expanse and discover their own secluded spot.

The cerulean waters of the Caribbean Sea gently lap against the shore, providing a refreshing backdrop for a day of relaxation or water-based activities. The calm and shallow nature of the water makes Valley Church Beach ideal for swimming, wading, and even snorkeling, especially around the rocky outcrops where marine life thrives.

Tranquil Atmosphere:

Unlike some of the more bustling beaches in Antigua, Valley Church Beach maintains a tranquil atmosphere. It's an excellent choice for those seeking a peaceful retreat or a romantic escape. The absence of large crowds allows visitors to fully immerse themselves in the natural beauty of the surroundings, creating a serene ambiance that enhances the overall experience.

Sunset Serenity:

Valley Church Beach is renowned for its spectacular sunset views. As the day draws to a close, the sky transforms into a canvas of warm hues, casting a golden glow over the beach. Sunset-seekers often gather on the sand or at one of the beachfront establishments to witness this breathtaking display of nature. It's a moment of serenity and romance that encapsulates the allure of the Caribbean.

Beachfront Amenities:

While Valley Church Beach exudes a sense of untouched paradise, it doesn't lack in modern amenities. Visitors can find beachfront establishments offering refreshments, snacks, and even full-service dining. Loungers and umbrellas are available for rent, providing a comfortable haven for those looking to spend the day by the sea.

Water Sports and Activities:

For the more adventurous souls, Valley Church Beach offers a range of water sports and activities. Local vendors provide opportunities for jet-skiing, paddleboarding, and even parasailing, allowing visitors to add an element of excitement to their beach day.

Nearby Attractions:

Valley Church Beach is not only a destination in itself but also a gateway to exploring nearby attractions. Jolly Harbour, with its marina, shops, and restaurants, is just a stone's throw away. A leisurely stroll along the coast can lead visitors to other hidden gems, including secluded coves and viewpoints.

Responsible Tourism:

Antigua and Barbuda take pride in their commitment to sustainable and responsible tourism. Visitors to Valley Church Beach are encouraged to respect the natural environment, follow designated pathways, and adhere to responsible beach etiquette. By doing so, tourists contribute to the preservation of this pristine paradise for generations to come.

Local Culture and Interaction:

Engaging with the local community around Valley Church Beach provides an opportunity to experience the warm hospitality and vibrant culture of Antigua. Local vendors may offer handmade crafts, providing visitors with souvenirs that reflect the artistic traditions of the island.

Planning Your Visit:

When planning a visit to Valley Church Beach, it's advisable to check weather conditions, especially during the hurricane season from June to November. Additionally, sunscreen, hats, and protective clothing are recommended to shield against the Caribbean sun. Visitors should carry sufficient cash for any beachfront services or local purchases.

3.11 Green Island:

Green Island, a pristine gem nestled in the azure waters surrounding Antigua and Barbuda, stands as a testament to the untouched beauty that the Caribbean archipelago has to offer. As a must-visit destination for tourists seeking tranquility, natural wonders, and an escape from the bustling world, Green Island beckons with its secluded beaches, vibrant marine life, and lush landscapes.

Geographical Splendor:

Located off the eastern coast of Antigua, Green Island is a captivating haven accessible by boat, offering visitors a picturesque journey across the clear, turquoise waters of the

Caribbean Sea. The island is characterized by its lush greenery, sandy shores, and a feeling of remoteness that adds to its allure.

Beach Bliss:

Green Island is renowned for its pristine beaches, where soft, powdery sands meet the gentle lapping of crystal-clear waves. Visitors are welcomed by the idyllic surroundings, providing the perfect setting for relaxation, sunbathing, and enjoying the breathtaking views. The beaches on Green Island are relatively untouched, providing an authentic and unspoiled Caribbean experience.

Snorkeling and Diving Paradise:

One of the primary draws of Green Island is its vibrant underwater world. The surrounding coral reefs teem with marine life, creating an underwater paradise for snorkelers and divers alike. The clarity of the water allows for exceptional visibility, offering glimpses of colorful coral formations, tropical fish, and other fascinating sea creatures. Snorkeling gear is a must for those looking to explore the rich biodiversity beneath the surface.

Boat Tours and Excursions:

To fully appreciate the beauty of Green Island and its surrounding waters, many tourists opt for boat tours and excursions. Various operators offer guided trips, providing insights into the local marine ecology and the history of the region. These excursions often include stops for snorkeling, allowing participants to immerse themselves in the captivating underwater realm.

Birdwatching Haven:

Green Island serves as a sanctuary for bird enthusiasts, providing a habitat for various avian species. Birdwatchers can spot seabirds, shorebirds, and even migratory species, creating a unique opportunity to connect with the diverse birdlife that calls the Caribbean home.

Picnics and Nature Walks:

Green Island invites visitors to embrace the laid-back Caribbean lifestyle. Many choose to pack a picnic and spend a leisurely day on the island's shores. Nature walks along designated trails offer a chance to explore the interior, discovering indigenous flora and fauna while taking in panoramic views of the surrounding seascape.

Secluded Retreats:

For those seeking a more intimate and private experience, Green Island provides a few secluded retreats. These accommodations, often in the form of beachfront cottages or eco-friendly resorts, offer a peaceful escape surrounded by nature. Staying on the island allows guests to enjoy its beauty at their own pace, with the sound of the waves as their constant companion.

Conservation Efforts:

Green Island is not only a natural wonder but also a testament to the importance of conservation. Efforts have been made to preserve the island's delicate ecosystem and protect it from the impacts of excessive tourism. Visitors are encouraged to respect the environment, follow responsible tourism practices, and contribute to the preservation of this pristine paradise.

How to Reach Green Island:

Access to Green Island is primarily by boat. Various tour operators and boat charters offer excursions from Antigua, providing transportation to and from the island. The boat journey itself is a delightful experience, with panoramic views of the coastline and the anticipation of reaching this secluded paradise.

Planning Tips for Visitors:

- Boat Tours and Excursions: Research and book boat tours or excursions in advance to secure a spot, especially during peak tourist seasons.
- Snorkeling Gear: Bring your own or check with tour operators to ensure they provide snorkeling gear for underwater exploration.
- Picnic Essentials: If planning a day trip, pack essentials such as sunscreen, water, snacks, and a picnic lunch to fully enjoy the beach experience.
- Conservation Awareness: Respect the natural environment by adhering to Leave No Trace principles and supporting conservation efforts on the island.

3.12 Barbuda's Pink Sand Beach:

This iconic beach stands as one of the most enchanting and sought-after destinations in Antigua and Barbuda, offering visitors a tranquil oasis of natural beauty.

A Beach Like No Other:

Renowned for its unique and mesmerizing pink sand, this beach is a testament to the wonders of nature. The distinct pink hue is derived from the abundance of crushed coral and shells, creating a picturesque contrast against the turquoise waters of the Caribbean Sea. The result is a breathtaking blend of colors that captivates every visitor fortunate enough to experience its allure.

Getting There:

Barbuda, located just a short boat ride or a quick flight from Antigua, is a haven for those seeking a serene escape. Pink Sand Beach, situated on the island's western coast, is easily accessible by boat or a short drive from the capital, Codrington. Visitors can arrange boat tours from Antigua or take a local flight to Barbuda's Codrington Airport, followed by a scenic drive to the beach.

Tranquil Serenity:

Upon arrival at Pink Sand Beach, you are welcomed by a sense of tranquility that sets the tone for a truly rejuvenating experience. The beach is less developed compared to its counterparts on Antigua, offering a more secluded and intimate setting. The absence of large crowds allows visitors to bask in the serenity of this natural paradise, making it an ideal spot for relaxation and contemplation.

Activities and Leisure:

While Pink Sand Beach is celebrated for its peaceful ambiance, there is no shortage of activities for those seeking a bit of adventure. Snorkeling enthusiasts can explore the vibrant coral reefs just offshore, encountering a kaleidoscope of marine life beneath the crystal-clear waters. The gentle waves make swimming a delight, and the beach's powdery sands provide the perfect canvas for a leisurely stroll.

Frigate Bird Sanctuary:

Adjacent to Pink Sand Beach lies another gem of Barbuda – the Frigate Bird Sanctuary. This ecological marvel is home to the largest frigate bird colony in the Western Hemisphere. Visitors can embark on guided tours to witness these majestic birds in their natural habitat, observing their distinctive mating rituals and soaring flights against the backdrop of Barbuda's lush landscape.

Picnics and Sunset Bliss:

For a more immersive experience, consider packing a picnic and savoring a delightful meal on the beach. The sound of gentle waves, the caress of the Caribbean breeze, and the stunning pink hues of the sand create an idyllic setting for a romantic getaway or a memorable family outing. As the day draws to a close, Pink Sand Beach transforms into a canvas of warm hues during sunset, providing an unforgettable spectacle for those fortunate enough to witness it.

Local Cuisine and Refreshments:

Exploring the local culinary scene is an essential part of any travel experience, and Pink Sand Beach doesn't disappoint. Visitors can indulge in freshly prepared seafood and traditional Caribbean dishes at nearby eateries, enhancing the overall beachside experience. Don't miss the opportunity to savor the flavors of the islands while enjoying the breathtaking views of the beach.

Preserving Barbuda's Natural Heritage:

Barbuda, known for its commitment to environmental conservation, has taken measures to protect Pink Sand Beach and its surrounding ecosystems. Visitors are encouraged to respect the natural environment by adhering to designated paths, refraining from disturbing wildlife, and properly disposing of waste. This collective effort ensures that future generations can continue to revel in the pristine beauty of this remarkable beach.

Accommodations and Nearby Attractions:

While Pink Sand Beach exudes tranquility, accommodations are available for those wishing to extend their stay on the island. Options range from charming guesthouses to luxury resorts, each offering a unique perspective of Barbuda's hospitality. Exploring nearby attractions, such as the Codrington Lagoon and Darby's Cave, provides additional opportunities to delve into the island's natural wonders.

Planning Your Visit:

To make the most of your experience at Pink Sand Beach, consider planning your visit during the dry season, from December to April, when the weather is optimal for beach activities and outdoor exploration. Additionally, checking local tide schedules can enhance your snorkeling experience and help you make the most of the crystal-clear waters.

3.13 Nonsuch Bay:

Nonsuch Bay stands as a hidden gem on the eastern coast of Antigua, inviting tourists to indulge in a serene and captivating retreat away from the bustling tourist hotspots. This pristine bay offers a unique blend of natural beauty, water activities, and luxurious accommodations, making it a must-visit destination for those seeking an idyllic Caribbean escape.

Nonsuch Bay Overview:

Nonsuch Bay is situated on the eastern side of Antigua, renowned for its tranquility and unspoiled landscapes. The bay is embraced by lush hills, providing a picturesque backdrop to its turquoise waters. What sets Nonsuch Bay apart is its secluded ambiance, offering visitors a serene haven away from the more bustling areas of the island.

Accommodations:

Several high-end resorts and accommodations grace the shores of Nonsuch Bay, each providing a unique blend of luxury and natural beauty. Resorts like Nonsuch Bay Resort and The Escape at Nonsuch Bay offer exclusive settings for visitors to unwind in style. Overlooking the bay, these establishments provide stunning views, private beaches, and upscale amenities that create a perfect balance of comfort and natural beauty.

Water Activities:

One of the highlights of Nonsuch Bay is its vast playground for water enthusiasts. The bay's calm and protected waters make it an ideal location for various water activities. Guests can engage in sailing, windsurfing, and kayaking, with the resort facilities often providing equipment and professional instructors for those looking to try these activities for the first time.

The Nonsuch Bay Resort is particularly known for its sailing school, which caters to all skill levels. Visitors can learn the ropes of sailing in the bay's gentle breezes, surrounded by the stunning Caribbean scenery. The resort's professional instructors ensure a safe and enjoyable experience for beginners while offering challenges for more experienced sailors.

Snorkeling and Diving:

The underwater world of Nonsuch Bay is equally captivating. Snorkeling enthusiasts can explore the coral reefs teeming with colorful marine life. The bay's clear waters provide excellent visibility, allowing snorkelers to witness vibrant coral formations and an array of tropical fish. For those seeking a more immersive experience, the resort often arranges diving excursions to nearby dive sites, unveiling Antigua's rich marine biodiversity.

Culinary Delights:

Nonsuch Bay doesn't just captivate with its natural beauty; it also indulges visitors with exquisite culinary offerings. The resorts within the bay often boast restaurants serving a blend of international and local cuisine. Guests can savor delectable dishes while enjoying panoramic views of the bay and surrounding landscapes. This culinary journey is complemented by the warm and welcoming atmosphere that characterizes the dining experiences in Nonsuch Bay.

Excursions and Day Trips:

Exploring beyond the bay unveils a myriad of opportunities for day trips and excursions. The nearby Green Island, accessible by boat, presents a pristine natural environment where visitors can enjoy secluded beaches and snorkeling in unspoiled coral reefs. Additionally, a short trip to Devil's Bridge, a natural limestone arch formation on the eastern coast, provides a unique geological marvel and an excellent vantage point for observing the Atlantic waves crashing against the rocks.

Local Insights:

Engaging with the local community offers a more authentic experience of Nonsuch Bay. Residents often share their knowledge of the area's history, traditions, and hidden gems. Exploring nearby villages allows visitors to witness the daily life of Antiguans, providing cultural insights and fostering connections that go beyond the typical tourist experience.

Wellness and Relaxation:

Nonsuch Bay is not only a haven for adventure seekers but also a retreat for those seeking relaxation and wellness. Many resorts in the area offer spa facilities where guests can indulge in rejuvenating treatments amidst the tranquil surroundings. Yoga sessions overlooking the bay or massage therapies with the soothing sounds of the Caribbean Sea create an atmosphere of ultimate relaxation.

3.14 Hawksbill Turtle Preserve:

This dedicated sanctuary, located on the northwest coast of Antigua, is a must-visit destination for tourists seeking an immersive and educational experience with these majestic sea creatures.

Discovering the Hawksbill Turtle:

The Hawksbill Turtle, scientifically known as Eretmochelys imbricata, is a critically endangered species that finds refuge in the warm Caribbean waters surrounding Antigua. Known for their strikingly beautiful shells and distinctively shaped beaks, these turtles have been an integral part of the region's marine ecosystem for centuries. The Hawksbill Turtle Preserve serves as a safe haven for these incredible creatures, offering them protection during nesting and nurturing periods.

Preservation Efforts:

Established as part of Antigua and Barbuda's commitment to biodiversity conservation, the Hawksbill Turtle Preserve is a designated area where these turtles can nest, lay eggs, and flourish without the threat of human interference. The preservation efforts are crucial in safeguarding the Hawksbill Turtle population, allowing them to contribute to the delicate balance of marine life in the Caribbean.

Nesting Season and Guided Tours:

The nesting season for Hawksbill Turtles typically occurs between June and November. During this period, the Hawksbill Turtle Preserve becomes a hub of activity as these ancient mariners return to the shores of Antigua to lay their eggs. Guided tours are available for visitors to witness this awe-inspiring natural phenomenon. Knowledgeable guides provide insights into the turtles' behavior, nesting habits, and the conservation efforts in place to protect these endangered species.

Turtle Hatchlings and Release Programs:

One of the most enchanting experiences at the Hawksbill Turtle Preserve is witnessing the hatching of turtle eggs and the subsequent release of the adorable hatchlings into the sea. Preservation programs work diligently to monitor and protect turtle nests, ensuring a high rate of successful hatching. Visitors fortunate enough to witness a hatching event are treated to a heartwarming display of nature's resilience.

Educational Initiatives:

The Hawksbill Turtle Preserve doesn't just offer a visual spectacle; it also serves as an educational hub, providing valuable insights into the importance of marine conservation. Visitors can engage in informative sessions led by marine biologists and conservationists, delving into the life cycle of Hawksbill Turtles, the challenges they face, and the broader implications of preserving biodiversity in the Caribbean.

Responsible Tourism Practices:

Tourists visiting the Hawksbill Turtle Preserve are encouraged to practice responsible and sustainable tourism. This includes adhering to designated paths during guided tours, refraining from touching or disturbing nesting sites, and respecting the natural habitat of these incredible creatures. By adopting responsible tourism practices, visitors play a crucial role in contributing to the long-term success of conservation efforts.

Snorkeling and Underwater Exploration:

For those seeking a more immersive experience, the Hawksbill Turtle Preserve offers snorkeling opportunities in designated areas. Under the guidance of experienced instructors, visitors can explore the vibrant underwater world where Hawksbill Turtles gracefully glide through the crystal-clear waters. Snorkeling adventures provide a unique perspective, allowing tourists to witness these marine marvels in their natural habitat.

Conservation Challenges and Community Involvement:

While the Hawksbill Turtle Preserve has made significant strides in conservation, challenges persist. Climate change, pollution, and habitat degradation are ongoing threats to these magnificent creatures. Recognizing the need for collective action, the preserve actively involves local communities in its conservation initiatives. Educational programs, community outreach, and collaborative efforts aim to foster a sense of shared responsibility for the protection of Hawksbill Turtles.

Planning Your Visit:

For tourists eager to include the Hawksbill Turtle Preserve in their Antigua and Barbuda itinerary, it's advisable to check with local conservation authorities for the latest information on guided tours, nesting seasons, and snorkeling opportunities. Advance bookings for guided tours are recommended, as these experiences are often in high demand, especially during nesting and hatching seasons.

3.15 Antigua Distillery:
The Distillery Experience:

1. Discovering the Art of Rum Making:

The Antigua Distillery, located on the outskirts of St. John's, provides an immersive experience into the age-old craft of rum production. Visitors are guided through the various stages of rum-making, from the sourcing of the finest sugarcane to the intricate processes of fermentation and distillation. The knowledgeable staff shares insights into the history of rum on the islands, painting a vivid picture of the integral role this spirit has played in Antigua's cultural tapestry.

2. Historical Significance:

The distillery itself is a testament to the historical significance of rum in the Caribbean. Housed within a charming colonial-era building, the Antigua Distillery exudes an old-world charm that resonates with the island's past. As visitors explore the facility, they gain a profound understanding of how rum production has evolved over the centuries, shaping the identity of the region.

Tasting Sessions:

1. A Connoisseur's Delight:

No visit to the Antigua Distillery is complete without indulging in a rum tasting session. The distillery boasts an impressive selection of aged rums, each with its own distinctive flavor profile. From the smooth and mellow notes of the 5-year-old blends to the complexity of the aged reserves, visitors have the opportunity to savor the craftsmanship of Antiguan rum production. Knowledgeable guides lead the tasting sessions, providing insights into the nuances of each blend and educating visitors on the art of rum appreciation.

2. Signature Cocktails:

For those seeking a more dynamic experience, the distillery's bar serves up an array of signature cocktails crafted with their premium rums. From classic mojitos to innovative concoctions that showcase the versatility of rum, the bar provides a lively atmosphere for socializing and enjoying the vibrant spirit of the Caribbean.

Interactive Workshops:

1. Blend Your Own Rum:

An exciting feature of the Antigua Distillery is its interactive workshops, allowing visitors to try their hand at blending their own personalized bottle of rum. Under the guidance of expert blenders, participants select from a variety of aged rums, experiment with different proportions, and create a bespoke blend to take home as a unique memento of their Antiguan experience.

2. Culinary Pairings:

The distillery also offers workshops that explore the art of pairing rum with culinary delights. Participants delve into the world of flavor harmonies as they sample various rums alongside carefully curated dishes. This gastronomic adventure provides a holistic understanding of rum's versatility in complementing diverse cuisines.

Distillery Gift Shop:

1. Exclusive Souvenirs:

Before concluding the visit, tourists can explore the distillery's gift shop, where an array of exclusive rum-related merchandise awaits. From elegantly packaged bottles of aged rum to branded glassware and accessories, the shop offers the perfect opportunity to bring home a piece of Antiguan rum culture.

Practical Tips for Visitors:

1. Tour Schedules and Reservations:

It is advisable to check the distillery's tour schedules in advance and make reservations, especially during peak tourist seasons. This ensures a personalized and unhurried experience.

2. Comfortable Attire:

The distillery tour may involve some walking, so wearing comfortable attire and footwear is recommended. Additionally, the tropical climate of Antigua suggests dressing appropriately for the weather.

3. Designated Drivers:

For those participating in tasting sessions, arranging transportation or having a designated driver is crucial. The distillery prioritizes responsible consumption and encourages visitors to enjoy their experience safely.

3.16 Hermitage Bay:

Nestled on the western coast of Antigua, Hermitage Bay stands as a testament to luxury, tranquility, and natural beauty. This secluded and exclusive resort encapsulates the essence of an idyllic Caribbean escape, making it a must-visit destination for tourists seeking a serene retreat in Antigua and Barbuda.

Location and Setting:

Situated on the pristine shores of Hermitage Bay, this five-star resort offers a secluded haven surrounded by lush hills and overlooking the crystal-clear waters of the Caribbean Sea. The location ensures a sense of exclusivity and privacy, making it an ideal choice for travelers seeking a romantic getaway, a peaceful retreat, or a luxurious escape.

Accommodations:

Hermitage Bay boasts luxurious and thoughtfully designed accommodations that seamlessly blend with the natural surroundings. The resort features individual cottages scattered along the hillside, each offering breathtaking views of the bay and ensuring an intimate and private experience. With open-air living spaces, private plunge pools, and direct access to the beach, guests can immerse themselves in the beauty of the Caribbean while enjoying the utmost comfort and seclusion.

Dining Experience:

The culinary experience at Hermitage Bay is nothing short of exceptional. The resort's restaurant, set against the backdrop of the bay, serves a delectable array of locally inspired dishes prepared with fresh, organic ingredients. Guests can savor the flavors of the Caribbean while enjoying panoramic views of the sunset. The all-inclusive package at Hermitage Bay includes gourmet meals, ensuring a delightful culinary journey throughout the stay.

Wellness and Spa:

For those seeking relaxation and rejuvenation, the resort's spa offers a range of holistic treatments inspired by traditional Caribbean practices. Nestled within a lush garden, the spa provides a serene and tranquil setting for guests to indulge in massages, facials, and wellness therapies. The use of natural and locally sourced ingredients adds an authentic touch to the spa experience.

Activities and Excursions:

While Hermitage Bay emphasizes tranquility, guests can also partake in a variety of activities to make the most of their Caribbean getaway. From water sports such as paddleboarding and kayaking to yoga sessions on the beach, the resort caters to a diverse range of interests. Additionally, the concierge can arrange personalized excursions for guests to explore the surrounding areas, including visits to historical sites, hiking trails, and boat trips to nearby islands.

Environmental Sustainability:

Hermitage Bay is committed to environmental sustainability and responsible tourism. The resort has implemented eco-friendly practices, including solar energy usage, water conservation initiatives, and support for local community projects. This dedication to sustainability aligns with the broader efforts in Antigua and Barbuda to preserve the natural beauty of the islands for future generations.

Romantic Escapes and Special Celebrations:

With its intimate setting and luxurious amenities, Hermitage Bay has become a sought-after destination for romantic escapes and special celebrations. The resort offers packages tailored for honeymooners, couples celebrating anniversaries, and those looking to create lasting memories in a romantic Caribbean setting. Private dining experiences on the beach, couples' massages, and personalized celebrations contribute to the allure of Hermitage Bay for romantic getaways.

Exclusive Events and Retreats:

Hermitage Bay also caters to those seeking an exclusive and private setting for events and retreats. The resort's facilities and attentive staff can accommodate weddings, corporate retreats, and other special gatherings, ensuring a seamless and memorable experience for all attendees.

Tips for a Hermitage Bay Experience:

- Book in Advance: Due to its exclusive nature, Hermitage Bay often has limited availability. Booking well in advance ensures that you secure your preferred dates and accommodations.

- Pack Light: The resort's casual and relaxed atmosphere allows for a light packing approach. Comfortable beachwear, swimwear, and resort casual attire are suitable for most occasions.
- Explore Antigua: While Hermitage Bay provides a tranquil sanctuary, take the opportunity to explore the broader beauty of Antigua. The resort's concierge can arrange guided tours, island excursions, and visits to local attractions.
- Embrace Wellness: Make the most of the spa and wellness offerings. Consider booking treatments in advance and incorporating yoga or meditation into your daily routine for a truly rejuvenating experience.
- Savor Local Flavors: The resort's culinary offerings showcase the best of Caribbean cuisine. Don't miss the chance to try local dishes and savor the flavors of the region during your stay.

3.17 Darkwood Beach:

Nestled on the southwestern coast of Antigua, Darkwood Beach stands as a serene oasis, inviting tourists to bask in the beauty of sun-kissed shores, pristine white sands, and the mesmerizing hues of the Caribbean Sea. Renowned for its tranquility and breathtaking scenery, Darkwood Beach has rightfully earned its place as a must-visit destination for those seeking a perfect blend of relaxation and natural splendor.

Location and Access:

Darkwood Beach is situated along the idyllic Fig Tree Drive, a scenic route that meanders through the lush landscapes of Antigua. The beach is conveniently located near Jolly Harbour, making it easily accessible for both independent travelers and those staying in the popular resort area. Whether you're driving or opting for a taxi, the journey to Darkwood Beach promises picturesque views and a taste of the island's vibrant greenery.

Natural Beauty and Seclusion:

What sets Darkwood Beach apart is its unspoiled natural beauty and a sense of seclusion. Enclosed by swaying palm trees and framed by verdant hills, the beach provides a tranquil escape from the hustle and bustle of busier tourist spots. The relatively low-key atmosphere makes it an ideal destination for those seeking a peaceful retreat and a genuine connection with nature.

The soft, powdery white sand underfoot is complemented by the gentle lull of the turquoise waters, creating a serene ambiance that captivates every visitor. Darkwood Beach's natural charm offers a stark contrast to the more commercialized areas on the island, making it a haven for those desiring an authentic Caribbean beach experience.

Swimming and Water Activities:

Darkwood Beach is not only about lounging on the sand; it beckons water enthusiasts with its calm and inviting waters. The gentle waves make it an excellent spot for swimming, and the gradual slope into deeper waters ensures accessibility for visitors of all ages. Snorkeling is also a popular activity here, as the crystal-clear waters reveal a vibrant underwater world teeming with colorful marine life.

For those seeking more adventurous activities, various water sports operators in the vicinity offer options like paddleboarding and kayaking. Exploring the shoreline from a different perspective enhances the overall experience, allowing visitors to embrace the full spectrum of Darkwood Beach's coastal beauty.

Local Vendors and Cuisine:

To complete the Darkwood Beach experience, visitors can indulge in the offerings of local vendors who dot the shoreline. Beachside shacks and stalls provide an array of refreshments, from tropical fruit platters to grilled seafood and refreshing beverages. The opportunity to savor authentic Caribbean flavors while lounging on the beach adds a delightful culinary dimension to the visit.

Engaging with the friendly locals and trying their delectable dishes offers a chance to immerse oneself in the island's culture. From freshly caught fish to coconut-infused treats, the culinary offerings at Darkwood Beach reflect the vibrant and diverse palette of Antiguan cuisine.

Scenic Hiking Opportunities:

For those who appreciate the allure of exploration, Darkwood Beach offers more than just a pristine shoreline. The surrounding hills and landscapes provide excellent hiking opportunities, with trails that lead to elevated vantage points offering panoramic views of the beach and the

Caribbean Sea beyond. The hike not only serves as a refreshing outdoor activity but also rewards participants with postcard-worthy vistas, making it a memorable addition to the Darkwood Beach experience.

Sunset Magic:

As the day transforms into evening, Darkwood Beach unveils another enchanting facet – its magical sunsets. The westward-facing beach becomes a canvas for the hues of the setting sun, casting a warm glow across the sea and the sky. Sunset-seekers often gather on the beach to witness this natural spectacle, creating a shared moment of awe and appreciation for the beauty that unfolds each evening.

3.18 Great Bird Island:

Nestled in the cerulean waters of the Caribbean, Great Bird Island stands as a hidden gem in Antigua and Barbuda's treasure trove of natural wonders. This secluded sanctuary, located just off the northeastern coast of Antigua, offers an unparalleled experience for nature enthusiasts and curious travelers seeking an escape into the pristine beauty of the Eastern Caribbean.

Getting There:

Embarking on a journey to Great Bird Island involves a scenic boat ride from Antigua's mainland. Numerous tour operators, both private and group, offer boat excursions to the island, allowing visitors to relish the panoramic views of the turquoise sea and the lush coastline. The boat ride itself becomes a prelude to the enchanting adventure that awaits on Great Bird Island.

Island's Flora and Fauna:

Great Bird Island, though petite in size, packs a punch when it comes to biodiversity. The island's lush vegetation, characterized by vibrant tropical flora, creates a verdant backdrop that complements the azure hues of the surrounding ocean. Walking along the well-maintained trails, visitors encounter an array of indigenous plant species, each contributing to the island's ecological tapestry.

True to its name, Great Bird Island is a haven for avian enthusiasts. The island hosts a diverse population of seabirds, including the red-billed tropicbird and the magnificent frigatebird. The frigatebird, with its distinctive silhouette and expansive wingspan, is a prominent resident and a delight for birdwatchers. As visitors explore the island's trails, they may witness these elegant creatures in their natural habitat, soaring gracefully overhead or nesting in the coastal vegetation.

Snorkeling in Pristine Waters:

One of the highlights of a visit to Great Bird Island is the opportunity to immerse oneself in the crystalline waters that surround it. The island is encircled by vibrant coral reefs teeming with marine life, making it an ideal spot for snorkeling enthusiasts. Visitors can don their snorkeling gear and explore the underwater realm, encountering colorful coral formations, tropical fish, and perhaps even sea turtles gliding gracefully through the sea.

The clear visibility and calm waters create an inviting atmosphere for both novice and experienced snorkelers. Guided snorkeling tours are also available, providing valuable insights into the marine ecosystem while ensuring a safe and enjoyable experience for all.

Picnic Paradise:

Great Bird Island beckons visitors to indulge in the simple pleasures of island life, making it an ideal spot for a leisurely picnic. The island is equipped with picnic tables and shaded areas, allowing guests to savor local delicacies amidst the breathtaking scenery. Whether it's a packed picnic basket or a catered meal from a tour operator, the experience of dining on Great Bird Island becomes a memorable blend of culinary delights and natural beauty.

Lighthouse Views:

Perched on the highest point of Great Bird Island is a charming lighthouse that adds a touch of maritime history to the landscape. The lighthouse, with its traditional design, provides panoramic views of the surrounding sea and neighboring islands. Climbing to the top offers a unique vantage point, allowing visitors to capture the essence of Antigua and Barbuda's coastal allure. The lighthouse, though functional, adds a nostalgic charm to the island and serves as a captivating landmark for those exploring its trails.

Conservation Efforts:

Great Bird Island stands as a testament to Antigua and Barbuda's commitment to environmental preservation. The island is a designated nature reserve, and efforts have been made to maintain its ecological balance while allowing responsible tourism. Conservation initiatives focus on protecting the island's flora and fauna, ensuring that future generations can continue to appreciate its natural beauty.

Visitors are encouraged to adhere to eco-friendly practices during their stay, such as avoiding the disturbance of wildlife and refraining from leaving any trace of their presence. By supporting sustainable tourism, guests contribute to the ongoing efforts to safeguard Great Bird Island's unique ecosystem.

Guided Tours and Nature Walks:

To maximize the Great Bird Island experience, many tour operators offer guided tours and nature walks. Knowledgeable guides lead visitors through the island's trails, sharing insights into its flora, fauna, and historical significance. These tours provide a deeper understanding of the island's ecological importance and showcase the delicate balance between conservation and tourism.

Nature walks often include stops at key points of interest, such as birdwatching areas, snorkeling spots, and the lighthouse. Guides may also share captivating anecdotes about the island's past, adding a layer of cultural richness to the natural exploration.

3.19 Museum of Antigua and Barbuda:

Visiting the Museum of Antigua and Barbuda is a captivating journey through time, offering tourists a deep dive into the rich and diverse history of these Caribbean islands. Nestled in the heart of St. John's, the capital city of Antigua, this museum stands as a cultural gem, providing a comprehensive overview of the islands' heritage from pre-Columbian times to the present day.

Exploring the Museum:

The Museum of Antigua and Barbuda, housed in the colonial-era Court House building, invites tourists to embark on a captivating exploration. The museum's exhibits are meticulously curated, offering a chronological narrative that unfolds through various artifacts, documents, and interactive displays.

Arawak and Carib Indigenous Peoples:

The journey begins with the indigenous peoples who inhabited the islands long before European colonization. Exhibits showcase the tools, pottery, and artifacts of the Arawak and Carib communities, providing insight into their daily lives and cultural practices. Intricately crafted items, such as ceremonial objects and pottery, offer a glimpse into the rich heritage of these early inhabitants.

European Colonization:

Moving forward in time, the museum delves into the era of European exploration and colonization. Displays highlight the arrival of Christopher Columbus in 1493 and the subsequent influence of the British on Antigua and Barbuda. Visitors can explore maps, navigational instruments, and colonial-era documents that shaped the islands' history.

Sugar Plantations and Slavery:

One of the pivotal chapters in Antigua and Barbuda's history is the era of sugar cultivation and slavery. The museum presents a sobering yet essential look at this period, featuring artifacts from the sugar plantations, including tools, documents, and remnants of the plantation system. Visitors gain a deeper understanding of the impact of slavery on the islands' development.

Emancipation and Independence:

The narrative progresses to the abolition of slavery and the eventual attainment of independence in 1981. Exhibits detail the struggles and triumphs of the islands' people during this transformative period. Important documents, photographs, and personal accounts provide a poignant reflection on the journey towards freedom and self-determination.

Cultural Celebrations:

The Museum of Antigua and Barbuda also highlights the vibrant cultural heritage of the islands through displays on Carnival and other traditional celebrations. Visitors can immerse themselves in the colorful costumes, music, and dance that define these cultural festivities.

Natural History and Marine Life:

Beyond human history, the museum dedicates space to the islands' natural history. Exhibits showcase the diverse flora and fauna unique to Antigua and Barbuda. Interactive displays provide information on the marine life found in the surrounding Caribbean waters, fostering an appreciation for the islands' ecological diversity.

Historic Architecture:

As visitors navigate through the museum, they can also explore the architectural history of Antigua and Barbuda. The building itself, the Court House, is a testament to colonial architecture and serves as a living relic of the islands' past. Its restoration and preservation add an extra layer of historical significance to the overall experience.

Practical Information for Visitors:

For tourists planning a visit to the Museum of Antigua and Barbuda, it's essential to note the operating hours and admission fees. The museum is generally open from Monday to Saturday, with slight variations in hours depending on the season. Admission fees are modest, with discounts available for students and seniors.

Guided tours are offered for those seeking a more in-depth exploration of the exhibits. Knowledgeable guides provide additional context, anecdotes, and insights, enriching the visitor experience. It's advisable to check the museum's official website or contact them directly for the latest information on operating hours and any special exhibitions or events.

Connecting with Local Culture:

A visit to the Museum of Antigua and Barbuda is not just a historical exploration but also an opportunity to connect with the local culture. The museum actively engages with the community, hosting events, workshops, and educational programs. Tourists interested in a more immersive experience can inquire about any ongoing events or activities during their visit.

Preserving the Islands' Heritage:

Beyond its role as a tourist attraction, the Museum of Antigua and Barbuda plays a crucial role in preserving and promoting the islands' heritage. The careful curation of exhibits, conservation efforts, and educational initiatives contribute to the ongoing narrative of Antigua and Barbuda. Tourists are encouraged to support these endeavors and gain a deeper appreciation for the importance of cultural preservation.

3.20 Fort James:

Nestled on the northern edge of the scenic St. John's Harbour, Fort James stands as a testament to Antigua and Barbuda's rich colonial history. This well-preserved military installation offers visitors a captivating journey back in time, providing a glimpse into the strategic importance of the Caribbean during the colonial era.

History and Significance:

Constructed in the early 18th century by the British, Fort James served as a vital defense post against potential invaders and marauders. Its strategic location overlooking St. John's Harbour allowed it to control the entrance to the bustling harbor, safeguarding the island from maritime threats. Named after King James II, the fort played a crucial role in protecting the interests of the British Crown in the Caribbean.

Architectural Marvels:

Fort James showcases a distinctive military architecture of the period, characterized by sturdy stone walls, gun emplacements, and a classic star-shaped design. The star-shaped layout, a common feature in European military engineering of the time, provided optimal coverage for defending against attacks from various angles. Visitors can explore the intricate network of tunnels, barracks, and vantage points within the fort, gaining insights into the challenges faced by the soldiers who once manned its defenses.

Panoramic Views:

One of the standout features of Fort James is its commanding views of St. John's Harbour and the surrounding coastline. The elevated position offers panoramic vistas of the azure Caribbean Sea, providing a picturesque backdrop for those looking to capture memorable photographs. Visitors often find themselves captivated by the juxtaposition of the historic fort against the modern skyline of St. John's.

Historical Exhibits and Interpretation:

Within the fort, informative exhibits and interpretative displays detail the history of Antigua and Barbuda during the colonial period. From the challenges faced by the early settlers to the pivotal role the fort played in naval operations, these exhibits offer a comprehensive understanding of the island's past. Knowledgeable guides are often available to provide additional context and share intriguing anecdotes, bringing the history of Fort James to life.

Cultural Events and Festivals:

Fort James also serves as a venue for various cultural events and festivals throughout the year. Visitors fortunate enough to coincide their trip with these festivities can experience the vibrant local culture against the backdrop of this historical site. From live music performances to traditional dance events, Fort James becomes a lively hub of cultural celebrations.

Sunset Celebrations:

One of the most enchanting experiences at Fort James is witnessing the breathtaking sunset over the Caribbean Sea. As the sun dips below the horizon, casting hues of orange, pink, and purple across the sky, the fort becomes a popular spot for locals and tourists alike to gather and celebrate nature's nightly spectacle. The rhythmic sounds of Caribbean music often accompany these sunset gatherings, creating a serene and memorable atmosphere.

Accessibility and Visitor Information:

Fort James is conveniently located near the heart of St. John's, making it easily accessible for tourists exploring the capital city. Many visitors choose to combine a visit to Fort James with a stroll through the historic streets of St. John's, taking in the vibrant markets, colonial-era architecture, and local shops.

For those interested in visiting Fort James, it's advisable to check for any special events or festivals scheduled during their stay. Guided tours are available for those seeking a more in-depth understanding of the fort's history, architecture, and cultural significance. Entrance fees are generally modest, and the experience is well worth the investment for history enthusiasts and anyone keen on immersing themselves in the captivating stories of Antigua and Barbuda's past.

3.21 Barbuda's Cave Pool:

For tourists seeking a truly extraordinary experience in Antigua and Barbuda, the journey to Barbuda's Cave Pool is a must. Nestled amid the island's stunning landscapes, this hidden gem offers a captivating blend of natural beauty and serene seclusion. Here, we delve into the enchanting allure of Barbuda's Cave Pool, guiding visitors through the journey to this extraordinary destination.

Introduction to Barbuda's Cave Pool:

Barbuda, the smaller sibling in the Antigua and Barbuda archipelago, is renowned for its pristine beaches and untouched natural splendor. However, hidden away from the more frequented tourist spots lies Barbuda's Cave Pool, an oasis of tranquility tucked within the heart of the island.

Location and Accessibility:

Situated in the midst of Barbuda's lush interior, reaching the Cave Pool requires a sense of adventure. While it's not directly on the beaten path, the journey is well worth the effort. Accessible primarily by guided tours or local guides, the route takes visitors through rugged terrain, providing glimpses of Barbuda's diverse landscapes.

The Cave Pool Experience:

Upon arrival, the Cave Pool unveils itself as a mesmerizing natural spectacle. The pool is nestled within a cave formed by ancient limestone rocks, creating a unique oasis of crystal-clear waters. The translucent pool is surrounded by the natural contours of the cave, offering a sense of seclusion and serenity.

Swimming in Nature's Embrace:

The allure of Barbuda's Cave Pool lies not only in its scenic beauty but also in the refreshing opportunity it provides for a swim in nature's embrace. The pristine waters are cool and inviting, creating a perfect setting for a leisurely swim or a moment of tranquil relaxation. The natural shade provided by the cave adds to the experience, making it an ideal spot to escape the Caribbean sun.

The Natural Formation:

The geological formation of the Cave Pool is a testament to the forces that have shaped Barbuda over time. The limestone rocks that encase the pool are a result of the island's unique topography, and the cave itself offers a glimpse into the ancient history of this Caribbean paradise. Exploring the nooks and crannies of the cave reveals the intricate details of nature's craftsmanship.

Flora and Fauna Surroundings:

Barbuda's Cave Pool is not just a geological wonder; it is also a haven for local flora and fauna. The surrounding areas are often rich with vibrant plant life, creating a lush backdrop for this natural sanctuary. Birdwatchers may find delight in the diverse avian species that inhabit the area, adding to the overall immersive experience of connecting with Barbuda's ecological diversity.

Guided Tours and Local Insights:

To make the most of the Cave Pool excursion, opting for guided tours or engaging local guides is highly recommended. Knowledgeable guides not only ensure a safe journey through the island's terrain but also provide valuable insights into the cultural and ecological significance of Barbuda's hidden gems. Learning about the folklore and history associated with the Cave Pool adds an extra layer of appreciation to the adventure.

Preserving the Natural Beauty:

Barbuda's Cave Pool is a testament to the delicate balance between tourism and environmental preservation. Visitors are encouraged to follow Leave No Trace principles, respecting the natural surroundings and minimizing their impact on this pristine environment. Preserving the integrity of the Cave Pool ensures that future generations can continue to marvel at this natural wonder.

Planning Your Visit:

For those eager to experience Barbuda's Cave Pool, proper planning is essential. Guided tours can be arranged through local tour operators or hotels, providing a structured and informative exploration of the island. As the Cave Pool is nestled away from the more frequented tourist spots, visitors should be prepared for a journey that involves some hiking and a sense of adventure.

What to Bring:

To make the most of the Cave Pool excursion, it's advisable to pack essentials such as sturdy hiking shoes, swimwear, a towel, sunscreen, and sufficient water. The terrain may be uneven, so comfortable footwear is crucial for the journey.

CHAPTER FOUR

NAVIGATING ANTIGUA AND BARBUDA

4.1 Transportation Options

When embarking on a journey to Antigua and Barbuda, understanding the transportation options available is crucial for a seamless and enjoyable experience. The twin islands offer a range of transportation choices catering to different preferences and travel needs.

4.1.1 Private Transportation:

For the discerning traveler seeking autonomy and convenience, private transportation in Antigua and Barbuda offers a personalized and flexible way to explore the stunning landscapes and vibrant culture of the twin islands.

Car Rentals:

Renting a car is a popular choice for those wishing to navigate the islands at their own pace. Several reputable car rental agencies operate at the airports and in major towns, providing a diverse range of vehicles to suit various preferences and group sizes. Tourists can choose from compact cars, SUVs, or even opt for a stylish convertible to add a touch of luxury to their island adventure.

Driving Regulations:

Antigua and Barbuda follows the British system of driving on the left side of the road. Tourists must possess a valid driver's license from their home country or an International Driving Permit to rent and drive a vehicle. It's essential to familiarize oneself with local traffic regulations, including speed limits and road signage, to ensure a safe and enjoyable driving experience.

Road Conditions:

The road network in Antigua and Barbuda is generally well-maintained, offering smooth and scenic drives across both islands. While major roads are paved and in good condition, some rural or off-the-beaten-path areas may have narrower roads. Travelers are encouraged to exercise caution, especially on less-traveled routes, and be mindful of local pedestrians and wildlife.

Fuel Stations:

Fuel stations are conveniently located throughout the islands, allowing tourists to refuel easily during their explorations. It's advisable to plan ahead and refuel when necessary, especially if venturing into more remote areas where fuel stations may be less frequent.

Parking Facilities:

Most tourist attractions, hotels, and popular destinations offer ample parking facilities. Tourists can safely park their rental vehicles while exploring beaches, historical sites, or enjoying dining experiences. It's recommended to confirm parking arrangements with accommodations in advance to ensure a hassle-free stay.

Benefits of Private Transportation:

The advantages of opting for private transportation are numerous. Travelers have the flexibility to create their itineraries, discover hidden gems off the beaten path, and enjoy the freedom of spontaneous stops. Private transportation is especially beneficial for those seeking a more intimate and personalized exploration of Antigua and Barbuda.

Exploring Remote Areas:

With private transportation, tourists have the opportunity to venture into remote and less touristy areas, unveiling the authentic charm of the islands. From secluded beaches to quaint villages, having a rental car allows visitors to go beyond the conventional tourist routes.

Convenience for Group Travel:

For families or groups traveling together, private transportation offers a convenient and cost-effective solution. It allows for easy coordination and ensures that everyone can travel together comfortably, maximizing shared experiences and minimizing logistical challenges.

Time Efficiency:

Private transportation enables visitors to make the most of their time on the islands. Without reliance on public schedules or group tours, tourists can optimize their itineraries, spending more time at preferred destinations and less time waiting for transportation.

Recommended Car Rental Agencies

1. Hertz Car Rental:

Location: V.C. Bird International Airport, St. John's, Antigua

Additional Locations: Hertz also has convenient rental counters in major towns such as St. John's and Jolly Harbour, providing easy access for tourists exploring different parts of Antigua.

2. Avis Car Rental:

Location: St. John's, Antigua

Additional Locations: Avis has a prominent presence in St. John's, the capital city, making it convenient for tourists arriving at the airport. They also have rental options in key tourist areas for seamless exploration.

3. Budget Car Rental:

Location: Sir George Walter Highway, St. John's, Antigua

Additional Locations: In addition to their airport location, Budget Car Rental has branches strategically situated in St. John's and other popular tourist hubs, offering diverse pick-up and drop-off options.

4. Thrifty Car Rental:

Location: Coolidge, St. John's, Antigua

Additional Locations: Thrifty Car Rental extends its services from the airport location to the heart of St. John's, ensuring tourists have accessibility to reliable transportation options no matter where their journey takes them on the island.

4.1.2 Taxis:

When it comes to convenient and reliable transportation in Antigua and Barbuda, taxis stand out as a popular and readily available option for tourists. Understanding the ins and outs of utilizing taxi services is key to ensuring a smooth and enjoyable experience while exploring the islands.

Availability:

Taxis are abundant at major tourist hubs, airports, and popular attractions, making them easily accessible for visitors. In towns and cities, you'll find taxi stands or designated areas where taxis wait for passengers. Additionally, many hotels can assist in arranging taxi services for guests.

Fares and Negotiation:

Unlike some destinations where taxis strictly operate on meters, in Antigua and Barbuda, it's common to negotiate fares with the driver before starting the journey. It's advisable to have an idea of the approximate fare for your intended route, and polite negotiation is a customary practice. Always confirm the fare with the driver before embarking on the trip.

Licensing and Identification:

Official taxis in Antigua and Barbuda are required to be licensed, and drivers should have proper identification. Look for a taxi with visible license plates, and the driver should display their driver's license upon request. This ensures that you are using a legitimate and regulated taxi service.

Shared Rides:

Shared taxi rides are a cost-effective option for travelers who don't mind sharing a cab with other passengers heading in the same direction. This practice is common, especially for shorter distances, and can be an opportunity to interact with fellow travelers.

Tourist Destinations:

Taxis are an excellent choice for reaching popular tourist destinations, including historic sites, beaches, and viewpoints. Drivers are often familiar with the main attractions and can provide valuable insights into local culture and history during your journey.

Airport Transfers:

Taxis are readily available at the airports in Antigua and Barbuda for hassle-free transfers to your accommodation. Drivers are accustomed to assisting tourists with their luggage, ensuring a smooth transition from the airport to your chosen destination.

Late-Night Travel:

Taxis are a reliable option for late-night travel, especially if you're returning to your accommodation after an evening of dining, entertainment, or exploring the vibrant nightlife. It's advisable to confirm availability and rates with your accommodation or the taxi stand in advance.

Payment Methods:

While some taxis accept credit cards, it's recommended to carry local currency for taxi fares, as not all drivers may have card payment facilities. Confirm the preferred payment method with the driver before starting your journey.

Safety Considerations:

Antigua and Barbuda maintain a generally safe environment, and taxis are a secure mode of transportation. However, it's always wise to exercise standard safety precautions. Inform someone about your destination, and if traveling alone, consider sitting in the back seat.

4.1.3 Public Buses:

Public buses in Antigua and Barbuda provide an authentic and budget-friendly means of exploring the islands, offering a unique glimpse into the daily life of the locals. Understanding the intricacies of the public bus system enhances the overall travel experience and allows tourists to traverse the islands with ease.

How to Identify Public Buses:

Public buses in Antigua and Barbuda are easily recognizable by their vibrant colors and distinctive markings. Look for buses painted in various shades, often adorned with local artwork or logos. Buses typically display their route numbers on the front windshield or side panels.

Bus Routes and Destinations:

Antigua's public bus system primarily operates along set routes, connecting major towns, popular tourist destinations, and local communities. Familiarizing yourself with the main routes ensures you can efficiently reach your desired location. Route maps are usually available at bus terminals or can be obtained from the local tourism office.

Bus Terminals and Stops:

Bus terminals are commonly found in major towns such as St. John's, where buses depart and arrive. Additionally, buses may have designated stops along their routes, making it convenient for passengers to board or alight. Pay attention to these stops and landmarks to navigate effectively.

Fares and Payment:

Bus fares in Antigua and Barbuda are generally reasonable, making public transportation an economical choice. It's advisable to carry local currency in small denominations, as exact change is preferred. Be prepared to pay the fare upon boarding, and some buses may not accept large bills.

Bus Schedule and Punctuality:

Public buses in Antigua and Barbuda operate on specific schedules. While the schedules are not as rigid as in some urban areas, it's advisable to check the timetable in advance. Buses may depart once they are full, so being punctual is recommended to secure a seat.

Interaction with Locals:

Engaging with locals during your bus journey can enhance the cultural experience. Antiguans are known for their friendliness, and striking up a conversation may lead to valuable insights, recommendations, or even new friendships. Respectful and courteous interactions contribute to a positive travel experience.

Seating and Etiquette:

Public buses may vary in terms of seating arrangements, ranging from standard bus seats to shared benches. It's customary to yield seats to elderly passengers or those with young children. Additionally, observe local etiquette, such as allowing others to exit before boarding.

Safety Considerations:

While public buses are generally safe, it's essential to take standard safety precautions. Keep an eye on your belongings, secure valuables, and be cautious when standing in crowded buses. Follow the guidance of the bus driver or conductor for a safe and pleasant journey.

4.2 Travel Safety Tips

Ensuring safety is paramount for any traveler exploring a new destination. In Antigua and Barbuda, a generally safe and welcoming environment awaits, but it's always prudent to adhere to travel safety guidelines.

1. Respect Local Customs and Laws:

Understanding and respecting local customs and laws is fundamental. Antigua and Barbuda have their own set of cultural norms and regulations, and visitors should familiarize themselves with these to avoid any unintentional breaches. For example, the possession of illegal substances can result in severe penalties.

1. Health Precautions:

Prioritizing health precautions contributes to a trouble-free vacation. Stay hydrated, especially in the tropical climate, and use sunscreen to protect against the sun's rays. Be cautious about food and water consumption to prevent any potential health issues. Having a basic medical kit with essentials like first aid supplies and personal medications is advisable.

3. Secure Your Belongings:

While both islands are generally safe, it's essential to practice common-sense security measures. Keep valuables secure, such as passports, travel documents, and electronic devices. Many accommodations provide safes for storing important items when not in use.

4. Emergency Contacts:

Familiarize yourself with local emergency contact numbers. Whether you need medical assistance, police support, or encounter any other emergency, having these numbers readily available ensures a prompt and effective response. Most accommodations provide this information, but it's wise to note it down for easy access.

5. Choose Accommodations Wisely:

Selecting safe and reputable accommodations is a key aspect of travel safety. Research and read reviews to choose hotels or guesthouses with positive feedback regarding security measures. Ensure that the chosen accommodation has secure access and well-lit premises.

6. Transportation Safety:

Whether using public transportation or renting a vehicle, prioritize transportation safety. Follow traffic rules if you choose to drive, wear seat belts, and be cautious on the roads. When using taxis, negotiate fares in advance, and choose reputable companies or drivers recommended by your accommodation.

7. Stay Informed about Local Conditions:

Stay updated on local conditions, weather forecasts, and any travel advisories that may affect your plans. Being aware of potential disruptions or natural events allows you to make informed decisions and ensures your safety during your stay.

8. Cultural Sensitivity:

Embrace cultural sensitivity to foster positive interactions with the local community. Dress modestly when visiting religious or rural areas, and ask for permission before taking photographs, especially of locals. Respectful behavior enhances your experience and promotes a harmonious relationship with the host community.

9. Trust Your Instincts:

Trusting your instincts is a valuable travel safety tip. If a situation feels uncomfortable or unfamiliar, remove yourself from it. Whether exploring the islands' natural wonders or engaging with locals, prioritizing your well-being ensures a memorable and secure visit.

4.3 Tips for Navigating Public Transportation

Exploring Antigua and Barbuda using public transportation can be an authentic and cost-effective way to experience the local culture. To make the most of this option, consider the following tips:

1. Learn the Routes:

Public buses typically follow set routes, and understanding the route map is crucial. Maps are often available at bus terminals or can be obtained from the local tourism office. Familiarize yourself with the main stops and destinations covered by the bus service.

2. Ask Locals for Guidance:

Engage with locals for insights on navigating public transportation effectively. Residents are often willing to provide helpful tips on bus routes, schedules, and any nuances specific to the area.

3. Be Mindful of Schedules:

Public transportation in Antigua and Barbuda may operate on specific schedules. It's advisable to check the bus timetable in advance to plan your journeys accordingly. Be punctual, as buses may adhere strictly to their schedules.

4. Have Exact Change:

When using public buses, having exact change can expedite the boarding process and ensure a smooth transaction. Bus fares are usually reasonable, and local currency is preferred for payment.

5. Stay Informed About Stops:

Pay attention to landmarks and key stops along the route to avoid missing your destination. Communicate with the bus driver or conductor to ensure they are aware of your intended stop.

4.4 Travel Insurance and its Importance

Understanding the importance of travel insurance ensures a secure and worry-free exploration of these idyllic twin islands.

1. Medical Coverage:

One of the primary reasons to prioritize travel insurance is for medical coverage. While Antigua and Barbuda boast excellent healthcare facilities, unexpected medical emergencies can happen. Travel insurance provides financial protection for medical expenses, hospitalization, and even medical evacuation if necessary. This coverage ensures that travelers can access quality healthcare without the burden of exorbitant costs.

2. Trip Cancellation or Interruption:

Life is unpredictable, and unforeseen events such as family emergencies, sudden illness, or natural disasters can disrupt travel plans. Travel insurance with trip cancellation or interruption coverage offers reimbursement for non-refundable expenses, including flights, accommodations, and pre-booked activities. This safeguards travelers from significant financial losses in case of unexpected disruptions.

3. Baggage and Personal Belongings:

While Antigua and Barbuda are generally safe, there's always a risk of lost, stolen, or damaged belongings during travel. Travel insurance provides coverage for baggage and personal items, offering financial assistance for the replacement or repair of items in such unfortunate situations. This ensures that travelers can continue their journey without undue stress.

4. Travel Delay or Missed Connections:

Delays are an inherent part of travel, whether due to weather, transportation issues, or other unforeseen circumstances. Travel insurance with coverage for travel delays or missed connections assists with additional expenses incurred during unexpected stopovers or delays. This includes accommodation, meals, and alternative transportation arrangements.

5. Emergency Assistance Services:

Opting for travel insurance with 24/7 emergency assistance services is a prudent choice. In the event of a medical emergency, travel disruption, or any unforeseen situation, having access to professional assistance can be invaluable. Emergency assistance services can provide guidance, coordinate medical care, and offer essential information during critical moments.

6. Adventure Activities Coverage:

Antigua and Barbuda offer a plethora of adventure activities, from water sports to hiking. It's crucial to ensure that travel insurance covers these activities, as some policies may have exclusions for high-risk endeavors. Having adequate coverage allows travelers to engage in thrilling experiences with the peace of mind that they are protected.

4.4.1 Types of Coverage to Consider

1. Medical Coverage:

One of the primary reasons for obtaining travel insurance is to cover medical expenses. Ensure that your policy includes coverage for medical emergencies, hospitalization, and medical evacuation. This is particularly important when visiting a destination where healthcare costs may be high.

2. Trip Cancellation or Interruption:

Unforeseen events such as family emergencies, illness, or natural disasters can disrupt travel plans. Trip cancellation or interruption coverage provides reimbursement for non-refundable expenses in such situations, allowing you to recoup some of the costs.

3. Baggage and Personal Belongings:

Travel insurance often includes coverage for lost, stolen, or damaged baggage. This ensures that you are financially protected in case your belongings are lost during transit or while staying in accommodations.

4. Travel Delay or Missed Connections:

Delays are an unfortunate part of travel. Whether due to weather, transportation issues, or other unforeseen circumstances, having coverage for travel delays or missed connections can provide assistance with additional expenses incurred during unexpected stopovers or delays.

5. Emergency Assistance Services:

Look for a travel insurance policy that offers 24/7 emergency assistance services. This can be invaluable in situations where immediate help or information is needed, such as medical emergencies or travel disruptions.

6. Adventure Activities Coverage:

If you plan to engage in adventure activities, such as water sports or hiking, ensure that your travel insurance covers these activities. Some policies may have exclusions for certain high-risk activities, so it's essential to review the terms carefully.

CHAPTER FIVE

ACCOMMODATION

5.1 Hotels and Resorts

Antigua and Barbuda, the enchanting twin islands in the Caribbean, boast a diverse array of hotels and resorts that cater to every traveler's desire for luxury, comfort, and impeccable service. These accommodations range from opulent beachfront resorts to charming boutique hotels, providing a range of options for visitors seeking a memorable stay.

Luxurious Beachfront Resorts:

Antigua and Barbuda are renowned for their world-class beachfront resorts, offering a perfect blend of luxury and natural beauty. These resorts, such as Jumby Bay Island and Hermitage Bay, provide an oasis of serenity with private villas, pristine beaches, and an array of amenities. Guests can indulge in spa treatments, gourmet dining, and breathtaking views of the Caribbean Sea.

Historic Elegance:

Some hotels in Antigua and Barbuda boast a rich history, with accommodations set within restored colonial-era buildings. These establishments, like Admiral's Inn and Copper and Lumber Store Hotel, offer guests the chance to immerse themselves in the islands' cultural heritage while enjoying modern comforts and unparalleled hospitality.

All-Inclusive Luxury:

For travelers seeking a hassle-free experience, all-inclusive resorts are abundant in Antigua and Barbuda. Resorts like Sandals Grande Antigua and Curtain Bluff provide comprehensive packages that cover accommodations, dining, and various activities. This approach allows guests to relax and enjoy their vacation without constantly managing expenses.

Recommended Hotels And Resorts With Their Locations

1. Jumby Bay Island

Location: Jumby Bay Island, Antigua

Description: A luxurious private island resort accessible only by boat, Jumby Bay Island offers an exclusive retreat with white sandy beaches, private villas, and world-class amenities. Surrounded by the crystal-clear waters of the Caribbean Sea, the resort provides a secluded paradise for discerning travelers.

2. Hermitage Bay

Location: Jennings New Extension, St. Mary's, Antigua

Description: Nestled on the west coast of Antigua, Hermitage Bay is a five-star, all-inclusive resort known for its breathtaking views, individual cottages with plunge pools, and exceptional service. Guests can enjoy a tranquil setting with direct access to the beach, gourmet dining, and a spa offering holistic treatments.

3. Carlisle Bay

Location: Old Road, St. Mary's, Antigua

Description: Situated on the southern coast of Antigua, Carlisle Bay is a luxury resort set against a backdrop of lush rainforest. The resort offers spacious suites with ocean views, a private beach, and an array of water activities. With contemporary design and a serene atmosphere, Carlisle Bay provides a sophisticated escape.

4. Curtain Bluff

Location: Old Road, St. Mary's, Antigua

Description: Perched on a picturesque bluff overlooking the Caribbean Sea, Curtain Bluff is an all-inclusive resort renowned for its elegant accommodations and exceptional service. With a private beach, championship tennis facilities, and a world-class spa, this resort offers a perfect blend of relaxation and recreation.

5. Cocobay Resort

Location: Valley Church Beach, St. Mary's, Antigua

Description: Cocobay Resort is a charming adults-only retreat located on the southwest coast of Antigua. Set amidst tropical gardens, the resort features colorful cottages with stunning sea views, two infinity pools, and a range of dining options. Cocobay offers a laid-back atmosphere and easy access to the white sands of Valley Church Beach.

5.2 Boutique Stays

In the realm of accommodations, boutique stays in Antigua and Barbuda stand out as unique, intimate, and full of character. These establishments prioritize personalized service, distinctive design, and a sense of immersion in the local culture, offering a charming alternative to traditional hotels.

Personalized Service and Attention:

Boutique stays pride themselves on delivering a level of personalized service that larger hotels often struggle to match. With fewer rooms and a focus on guest satisfaction, establishments like Sugar Ridge Hotel and The Inn at English Harbour create an environment where every guest feels valued and attended to, creating a homey atmosphere.

Distinctive Design and Atmosphere:

The design of boutique stays reflects the character of the destination, providing guests with a unique and immersive experience. From individually decorated rooms to locally inspired architecture, these accommodations, like Sugar Ridge Hotel and Keyonna Beach Resort, offer a distinctive charm that enhances the overall stay.

Recommended Boutique Stays With Their Locations

1. Sugar Ridge Hotel

Location: Jolly Harbour, St. Mary's, Antigua

Description: Tucked away on a hillside overlooking the Caribbean Sea, Sugar Ridge Hotel is a chic boutique stay with modern design and panoramic views. The hotel offers stylish rooms, a tranquil spa, and multiple dining options. Guests can enjoy the serenity of the location while being close to Jolly Harbour's amenities.

2. The Inn at English Harbour

Location: English Harbour, St. Paul's, Antigua

Description: Located near the historic English Harbour, this boutique hotel exudes colonial charm and sophistication. The Inn at English Harbour offers spacious suites and beachfront cottages surrounded by lush gardens. Guests can experience the tranquility of the Caribbean while being within reach of Nelson's Dockyard and other local attractions.

3. Keyonna Beach Resort

Location: Turner's Beach, St. Mary's, Antigua

Description: An intimate adults-only boutique resort, Keyonna Beach Resort is situated on the southwest coast, offering seclusion and romance. The resort features charming cottages with private verandas, direct beach access, and an open-air restaurant showcasing locally inspired cuisine.

4. The Great House Antigua

Location: Bolans Village, St. Mary's, Antigua

Description: A meticulously restored plantation house, The Great House Antigua provides a unique blend of history and luxury. Surrounded by lush gardens, the boutique stay offers elegantly appointed rooms, a swimming pool, and an authentic Caribbean dining experience. Guests can immerse themselves in the island's colonial heritage.

5. Yepton Estate Cottages

Location: Five Islands Village, St. John's, Antigua

Description: Nestled on a private estate near the shores of the Caribbean Sea, Yepton Estate Cottages offers self-catering boutique accommodations surrounded by tropical gardens. The charming cottages provide a peaceful retreat with easy access to nearby beaches and attractions, making it an ideal choice for those seeking a more independent stay.

5.3 Budget-Friendly Options

Antigua and Barbuda may be known for luxury, but there are also budget-friendly accommodation options for travelers seeking an affordable yet comfortable stay. These choices include local guesthouses, budget room categories in larger hotels, and self-catering options that provide flexibility without compromising on quality.

Local Guesthouses and Inns:

Antigua and Barbuda's local guesthouses and inns offer a friendly and budget-friendly atmosphere. Establishments like Caribbean Inn and Oceanic View Exclusive Vacation Cottages provide comfortable lodgings and personalized service, allowing guests to experience the warmth of Antiguan hospitality without breaking the bank.

Budget Room Categories in Larger Hotels:

Several larger hotels in Antigua and Barbuda offer budget room categories, providing affordable options within the confines of a resort setting. This allows budget-conscious travelers to enjoy the amenities and services of a larger hotel while maintaining cost-effective accommodations.

Self-Catering Options:

For those seeking flexibility in dining, self-catering options abound in Antigua and Barbuda. Vacation rentals, apartments, and cottages equipped with kitchens or kitchenettes, such as Yepton Estate Cottages, offer budget-conscious travelers the freedom to prepare their meals and manage expenses more efficiently.

Recommended Budget-Friendly Accommodation With Their Locations

1. Caribbean Inn

Location: Osbourn, St. George, Antigua

Description: Caribbean Inn is a budget-friendly accommodation located in Osbourn, offering comfortable rooms at affordable rates. The inn provides a warm and welcoming atmosphere, making it an excellent choice for budget-conscious travelers looking for a centrally located option with easy access to local amenities.

2. Oceanic View Exclusive Vacation Cottages

Location: Seatons Village, St. Philip's, Antigua

Description: Situated on the northeastern coast, Oceanic View Exclusive Vacation Cottages offers budget-friendly accommodations with breathtaking views of the Atlantic Ocean. The cottages are surrounded by tropical gardens, providing guests with a peaceful retreat while still being close to popular attractions.

3. Heritage Hotel

Location: Heritage Quay, St. John's, Antigua

Description: Heritage Hotel, located in the heart of St. John's, provides budget-friendly rooms with easy access to the capital's shopping, dining, and cultural attractions. The hotel offers a simple yet comfortable stay, making it a convenient choice for travelers exploring the vibrant city life.

4. Connie's Comfort Suites

Location: Potters Village, St. John's, Antigua

Description: Connie's Comfort Suites is a budget-friendly option situated in Potters Village. The hotel offers straightforward accommodations with essential amenities, making it suitable for travelers seeking affordable lodging with proximity to the capital and its surrounding areas.

5. Eko Cozy Guest House

Location: Cedar Valley Gardens, St. John's, Antigua

Description: Eko Cozy Guest House provides budget-friendly rooms in a tranquil setting. Located in Cedar Valley Gardens, this guest house offers a relaxed atmosphere with easy access to nearby beaches and natural attractions. It's an ideal choice for those looking for a simple and affordable stay in a peaceful environment.

5.4 Unique Accommodation Experiences

Antigua and Barbuda, with their captivating landscapes, offer a range of unique accommodation experiences that go beyond the ordinary. From charming beachside cottages to historic plantation houses, these distinctive stays promise travelers an unforgettable journey filled with authenticity and charm.

Charming Beachside Cottages:

Imagine waking up to the gentle sound of waves and stepping onto soft sands right outside your door. Charming beachside cottages in Antigua and Barbuda, like those at Dickenson Bay Cottages, provide an intimate and serene escape. These accommodations allow guests to immerse themselves in the natural beauty of the Caribbean while enjoying a cozy and private retreat.

Historic Plantation Houses:

Antigua's rich colonial history is reflected in its historic plantation houses, offering a unique blend of elegance and heritage. The Great House Antigua, beautifully restored and nestled in lush gardens, provides guests with the opportunity to step back in time while enjoying modern comforts and refined hospitality.

Recommended Unique Accommodation With Their Locations

1. Dickenson Bay Cottages

Location: Dickenson Bay, St. John's, Antigua

Description: Offering a unique and charming experience, Dickenson Bay Cottages provides beachside accommodations with direct access to the sandy shores of Dickenson Bay. The cottages offer a blend of intimacy and serenity, making it an ideal choice for travelers seeking a relaxed and distinctive stay on the northwest coast.

2. Ondeck Yacht

Location: Falmouth Harbour, St. Paul's, Antigua

Description: For a truly maritime experience, consider staying on the Ondeck Yacht located in Falmouth Harbour. This unique accommodation allows guests to enjoy the luxury of living on the water, surrounded by the picturesque scenery of the harbor. With the freedom to explore nearby bays and coves, the Ondeck Yacht offers an unparalleled maritime retreat.

3. The Treehouse at Sugar Ridge

Location: Sugar Ridge, St. Mary's, Antigua

Description: Nestled in the lush landscapes of Sugar Ridge, The Treehouse offers a unique treetop retreat with panoramic views of the Caribbean Sea. This elevated accommodation combines luxury with natural immersion, providing guests with a distinctive experience surrounded by the island's tropical flora and fauna.

5.5 Booking Accommodation in Advance

Planning a trip to Antigua and Barbuda involves strategic decision-making, and booking accommodation in advance is a key element of that process. Whether you're aiming for a luxurious resort, a charming boutique stay, or a budget-friendly option, securing your lodging early offers several advantages.

1. Ensuring Availability During Peak Seasons:

Antigua and Barbuda experience peak travel seasons, often coinciding with holidays and favorable weather conditions. Booking accommodation in advance ensures that you secure your preferred choice, especially during these periods when demand is high. This proactive approach helps you avoid the risk of limited availability or fully booked establishments.

2. Accessing Early Booking Discounts and Special Offers:

Many hotels and resorts in Antigua and Barbuda incentivize early bookings by offering discounts and special promotions. These can include reduced room rates, complimentary amenities, or exclusive package deals. Taking advantage of these offers not only helps you save money but also enhances the overall value of your stay.

3. Peace of Mind and Reduced Stress:

Booking your accommodation in advance provides peace of mind, eliminating the stress of last-minute searches for available rooms. Knowing that a crucial aspect of your trip is already taken care of allows you to focus on other aspects of your travel plans. This proactive approach contributes to a smoother and more enjoyable vacation experience.

4. Exploring Diverse Options Thoroughly:

Antigua and Barbuda offer a diverse range of accommodations, each with its own unique charm and features. By booking in advance, you have the luxury of thoroughly exploring your options, reading reviews, and choosing the type of lodging that aligns with your preferences and budget. Whether it's a beachfront resort, a boutique stay, or a budget-friendly guesthouse, early booking allows you to make an informed decision.

5. Tailoring Your Stay to Special Occasions:

If your trip coincides with a special occasion or celebration, booking in advance allows you to secure accommodations that cater specifically to these events. Some resorts may offer special packages or additional amenities for guests celebrating milestones, adding an extra layer of enjoyment to your stay.

6. Flexibility in Room Choices and Preferences:

Advance booking increases the likelihood of securing your preferred room type, whether it's a beachfront suite, a room with a panoramic view, or a more secluded accommodation. This ensures that you get the most out of your chosen lodging, aligning with your specific desires and enhancing the overall quality of your stay.

5.6 Tips for Finding the Right Lodging for Your Needs

Choosing the right lodging is a pivotal aspect of planning a successful and enjoyable trip to Antigua and Barbuda. With an abundance of options, including hotels, boutique stays, and budget-friendly accommodations, finding the perfect place to stay requires thoughtful consideration. Here are some tips to guide you in selecting the right lodging for your needs in the Caribbean paradise.

1. Define Your Priorities:

Before delving into the options, take a moment to define your travel priorities. Consider whether you prioritize luxury, cultural immersion, proximity to certain attractions, or a budget-friendly stay. Understanding your preferences will help narrow down your choices and make the decision-making process more straightforward.

2. Establish a Realistic Budget:

Antigua and Barbuda offer a range of accommodations catering to different budget levels. Before starting your search, establish a realistic budget for your stay. This will help filter out options that may be beyond your financial comfort zone and allow you to focus on choices that align with your budgetary constraints.

3. Research and Read Reviews:

Harness the power of online resources and reviews to gain insights into potential accommodations. Platforms like TripAdvisor, Booking.com, and travel forums provide valuable feedback from fellow travelers. Pay attention to aspects that align with your priorities and expectations, and be sure to read both positive and negative reviews for a balanced perspective.

4. Consider the Type of Accommodation:

Antigua and Barbuda offer a diverse array of accommodation types, from luxury resorts and boutique stays to budget-friendly guesthouses and self-catering options. Consider the type of experience you're seeking – whether it's a beachfront resort, an intimate boutique stay, or a more local and budget-friendly experience.

5. Check Location and Accessibility:

The islands' diverse landscapes offer different settings, from bustling urban areas to secluded beachfront locales. Consider the location of your accommodation in relation to the activities you plan to undertake. Whether you prefer a central location with easy access to amenities or a more secluded retreat, ensuring the accommodation aligns with your itinerary is crucial.

6. Explore Unique Features and Amenities:

Each accommodation in Antigua and Barbuda has its own unique features and amenities. Explore what makes each option stand out, whether it's a historic setting, beachfront access, or distinctive cultural offerings. Consider what features are essential to your stay and which ones align with your interests.

7. Look for Special Offers and Packages:

Many hotels and resorts in Antigua and Barbuda offer special packages and exclusive deals. These can include discounted rates, complimentary amenities, or additional perks. Be sure to check for any ongoing promotions that may enhance the value of your stay.

8. Consider Booking in Advance:

To secure your preferred lodging, especially during peak seasons, consider booking in advance. This not only ensures availability but may also provide access to early booking discounts and special offers. Planning ahead allows you to make a more informed decision and increases the likelihood of securing your ideal accommodation.

9. Contact the Accommodation Directly:

If you have specific questions or requests, don't hesitate to contact the accommodation directly. Whether it's regarding room preferences, special occasions, or any specific needs, direct communication allows you to clarify details and ensure that your stay meets your expectations.

CHAPTER SIX

DINING IN ANTIGUA AND BARBUDA

6.1 Must-Taste Dishes and Local Delicacies

Antigua and Barbuda offer a culinary journey that reflects the vibrant blend of African, British, and Caribbean influences. Exploring the local food scene is an essential part of experiencing the culture of these twin islands. Here are some must-taste dishes and local delicacies that will tantalize your taste buds:

1. Pepperpot: A hearty stew made with spinach, okra, eggplant, and meat (usually salted beef or pork), seasoned with a blend of spices. This dish is a delicious representation of the island's culinary heritage.

2. Fungi and Peppered Shrimp: Fungi, a cornmeal-based side dish, is often paired with succulent peppered shrimp. The combination of the spicy shrimp and the comforting texture of fungi creates a symphony of flavors.

3. Ducana: A sweet potato dumpling, grated and mixed with coconut, sugar, and spices, then wrapped in banana leaves and boiled. It's a delectable side dish often served with saltfish and seasoned meat.

4. Conch Salad: Embrace the Caribbean seafood experience with conch salad, a refreshing mix of diced conch, onions,

peppers, and citrus juices. The dish is typically seasoned with a hint of Scotch bonnet pepper for a spicy kick.

5. Jerk Chicken: Influenced by Jamaican cuisine, jerk chicken in Antigua and Barbuda is a flavorful delight. Chicken is marinated in a spicy jerk seasoning blend, then grilled to perfection, resulting in a smoky, spicy, and succulent dish.

6. Seafood Callaloo: A rich and savory soup featuring callaloo leaves, coconut milk, and an array of fresh seafood, including shrimp and crab. This dish showcases the abundance of seafood available in the surrounding Caribbean waters.

7. Black Pineapple: Sample the local black pineapple, a unique variety that is sweeter and juicier than its yellow counterparts. This tropical fruit is a refreshing treat, especially on a warm Caribbean day.

6.2 International Flavors

While embracing the local cuisine is a must, Antigua and Barbuda also offer a diverse array of international flavors to cater to every palate. The islands' culinary scene has evolved to include a range of international influences, ensuring that visitors can savor familiar tastes alongside the local fare.

Italian Cuisine:

Indulge in the flavors of Italy at various Italian restaurants across the islands. From handmade pasta to wood-fired pizzas, these establishments bring a touch of Mediterranean charm to the Caribbean. Picture yourself dining on a terrace overlooking the sea, savoring the rich and savory notes of a perfectly crafted bowl of pasta. Antigua and Barbuda's Italian eateries often source local ingredients, infusing a Caribbean twist into traditional Italian dishes. Whether you're in the mood for a classic Margherita pizza or a plate of al dente spaghetti, the Italian culinary offerings provide a delightful break from the local cuisine.

Asian Fusion:

Explore the fusion of Asian flavors with Caribbean ingredients. Restaurants offering sushi, Thai-inspired dishes, and other Asian delicacies provide a diverse culinary experience for those seeking an international twist. Imagine the fusion of Caribbean spices with the umami of sushi or the bold flavors of Thai cuisine. These establishments expertly blend the best of both worlds, creating a harmonious palate of tastes and textures. Whether you opt for a plate of expertly rolled sushi or indulge in a spicy Thai curry, the Asian fusion options on the islands offer a culinary journey that transcends borders.

French-Inspired Delights:

Experience the elegance of French cuisine at select restaurants, where classic dishes like coq au vin and bouillabaisse are reimagined with a Caribbean flair. Imagine dining in an intimate setting adorned with French-inspired decor, indulging in the exquisite flavors of a perfectly cooked coq au vin. French-inspired eateries in Antigua and Barbuda masterfully infuse local ingredients into traditional French recipes, creating a unique and delightful dining experience. From delicate pastries to savory stews, the influence of French culinary artistry adds a touch of sophistication to the islands' gastronomic landscape.

American Comfort Food:

For those craving a taste of home, numerous establishments serve American-style comfort food. From juicy burgers to crispy fried chicken, you'll find familiar favorites on the menu. Picture yourself enjoying a classic cheeseburger with a side of golden fries, or savoring the nostalgic taste of perfectly seasoned fried chicken. These American-inspired eateries offer a comforting haven for visitors seeking the familiar flavors of home amidst the tropical paradise of Antigua and Barbuda.

Mediterranean Delicacies:

Enjoy the light and flavorful dishes of the Mediterranean at restaurants that offer Greek, Turkish, or Spanish-inspired cuisine. Fresh seafood, olive oil, and aromatic herbs take center stage in these delightful dishes. Imagine dining in a seaside restaurant, relishing the taste of grilled octopus drizzled with olive oil or savoring a plate of paella with the backdrop of the Caribbean Sea. The Mediterranean-inspired offerings in Antigua and Barbuda bring a touch of the old world to the new, creating a culinary experience that transports you to the shores of the Mediterranean.

Indian Spice Sensations:

Spice up your culinary adventure with Indian-inspired flavors. Explore the aromatic curries, tandoori dishes, and rich spices that bring a taste of India to the Caribbean. Picture yourself savoring the complex flavors of a perfectly spiced curry or enjoying the smoky goodness of tandoori-marinated meats. Antigua and Barbuda's Indian-inspired eateries infuse the islands with the vibrant and diverse flavors of Indian cuisine. Whether you're a fan of creamy butter chicken or prefer the heat of a spicy vindaloo, the Indian spice sensations on the islands cater to a wide range of taste preferences.

6.3 Popular Markets and Local Market Adventures

Dive into the heart of the islands' vibrant culture by exploring the bustling markets, where the aromas of spices, the vibrant colors of fresh produce, and the lively atmosphere create an unforgettable experience.

St. John's Saturday Morning Market:

Start your market adventure at the St. John's Saturday Morning Market, a kaleidoscope of sights and sounds. The air is filled with the sweet fragrance of tropical fruits and the lively chatter of vendors and shoppers. This market is not just about shopping; it's a sensory celebration where locals and visitors alike come together. From exotic fruits like soursop and breadfruit to handcrafted souvenirs, the market offers a diverse array of goods. Engage with the vendors, learn about the cultural significance of their products, and savor the authenticity of the island's bustling market scene.

Redcliffe Quay Market:

Venture into the historic district of St. John's and discover the charm of Redcliffe Quay Market. This open-air market is a treasure trove of unique finds, featuring boutique shops and stalls showcasing local art, jewelry, and crafts. The market's colonial architecture provides a picturesque backdrop as you explore the narrow lanes lined with vibrant stalls. Take your time to browse through handmade textiles, traditional Antiguan crafts, and one-of-a-kind souvenirs that reflect the island's rich cultural heritage.

Heritage Quay:

For a different market experience, head to Heritage Quay, a duty-free shopping destination in St. John's. While it may be known for its luxury boutiques and international brands, Heritage Quay also features local vendors offering handmade crafts and souvenirs. This juxtaposition of global and local flavors creates a unique shopping experience. Take a leisurely stroll through the mall, where the aroma of freshly brewed coffee mingles with the scent of sea air, and explore the diverse range of goods on offer.

Potters Village Farmer's Market:

If you seek a more laid-back and authentic market adventure, venture to the outskirts of St. John's and discover the Potters Village Farmer's Market. Here, the pace is unhurried, and the atmosphere is infused with the spirit of community. Engage with local farmers, learn about traditional Antiguan agricultural practices, and sample fresh produce straight from the source. It's a wonderful opportunity to connect with the island's agricultural heritage and gain insights into the importance of locally sourced ingredients in Antiguan cuisine.

The Craft Market at Nelson's Dockyard:

Combine history with shopping at the Craft Market located at Nelson's Dockyard. This market, nestled within the historic surroundings of the dockyard, showcases the creativity of local artisans. Explore stalls offering handmade crafts, jewelry, and art inspired by Antigua and Barbuda's maritime history. As you peruse the offerings, you'll find unique pieces that reflect the skill and craftsmanship of the island's talented artists.

Barbuda's Local Markets:

When visiting Barbuda, immerse yourself in the local market scene, where the pace is unhurried, and the atmosphere reflects the tranquil charm of the island. Discover handmade baskets, woven crafts, and souvenirs that capture the essence of Barbuda's cultural identity. Engage in conversations with local artisans, and gain a deeper appreciation for the craftsmanship that goes into each piece.

6.4 Dining Etiquette

Understanding and respecting local dining etiquette is an integral part of immersing yourself in the culture of Antigua and Barbuda. Whether dining in a local eatery or an upscale restaurant, here are some essential dining etiquette tips to enhance your culinary experience:

1. Greetings and Respect: Begin your dining experience with a friendly greeting. It's customary to acknowledge staff and fellow diners with a warm "good morning," "good afternoon," or "good evening." Showing respect is a key element of Antiguan and Barbudan culture.

2. Casual Dress Code: While some upscale restaurants may have a dress code, many local eateries and beachfront establishments have a more casual atmosphere. Light,

comfortable clothing is often suitable for enjoying a meal on the islands.

3. Island Time: Embrace the relaxed pace of life in Antigua and Barbuda. Meals are an unhurried affair, and service may be more leisurely than in busier urban settings. Allow yourself to savor the experience and enjoy the laid-back island ambiance.

4. Seafood Etiquette: Given the abundance of seafood in local cuisine, it's helpful to be familiar with seafood etiquette. When dining on whole fish, it's common to debone the fish at the table, so don't be surprised if your server offers to do so.

5. Tipping Culture: Tipping is appreciated in Antigua and Barbuda, and it is customary to leave a gratuity of around 10-15% in restaurants. Some establishments may include a service charge, so check the bill before adding an additional tip.

6. Local Customs: Embrace the local customs when dining. It's customary to eat with the fork in the left hand and the knife in the right. When finished, placing your utensils parallel across the right side of the plate indicates that you are done.

7. Try Local Specialties: Don't hesitate to try local specialties and engage in conversation with locals to learn more about the dishes. Antiguans and Barbudans take pride in their culinary traditions, and expressing interest in the local cuisine is often met with enthusiasm.

By observing these dining etiquette tips, you'll not only enhance your culinary experience but also contribute to the warm and welcoming atmosphere that defines the hospitality of Antigua and Barbuda.

6.5 Recommended Restaurants with Their Locations

Exploring the diverse culinary landscape of Antigua and Barbuda involves discovering hidden gems and renowned establishments that showcase the best of local and international flavors. Here are some recommended restaurants, each offering a unique dining experience along with their respective locations:

1. Sheer Rocks (Cocobay Resort)

Location: Valley Church Beach, St. Mary's, Antigua

Cuisine: Mediterranean and Caribbean Fusion

Overview: Perched on a cliff overlooking the turquoise waters, Sheer Rocks offers an intimate dining experience. Indulge in a curated menu featuring Mediterranean-inspired dishes with a Caribbean twist. The romantic ambiance and stunning sunset views make it a must-visit for couples and those seeking a special culinary experience.

2. Cloggy's at the Antigua Yacht Club

Location: Falmouth Harbour Marina, English Harbour, Antigua

Cuisine: International, Seafood

Overview: Set against the backdrop of Falmouth Harbour, Cloggy's provides a relaxed atmosphere with a diverse menu.

From fresh seafood to international dishes, patrons can enjoy a delightful dining experience while taking in the picturesque views of the marina and yachts.

3. Papa Zouk Fish & Rum Bar

Location: Gambles Terrace, St. John's, Antigua

Cuisine: Seafood, Caribbean

Overview: A local favorite, Papa Zouk is a rustic fish and rum bar known for its laid-back vibe. Dive into an extensive menu of fresh seafood, complemented by an impressive selection of Caribbean rums. The casual setting and friendly atmosphere make it a popular choice among both locals and visitors.

4. The Cove Restaurant (Blue Waters Resort & Spa)

Location: Soldier's Bay, St. John's, Antigua

Cuisine: Caribbean, International

Overview: Located on the waterfront of Soldier's Bay, The Cove Restaurant offers an elegant dining experience. The menu features a blend of Caribbean and international cuisine, providing patrons with a taste of culinary excellence in a serene and picturesque setting.

5. Russell's Bar & Seafood Restaurant

Location: Jolly Harbour Marina, St. Mary's, Antigua

Cuisine: Seafood, Grill

Overview: Nestled in Jolly Harbour, Russell's is renowned for its seafood and grill specialties. Diners can enjoy al fresco seating on the waterfront terrace, savoring expertly prepared dishes while soaking in the laid-back atmosphere of the marina.

6. The Admiral's Inn (Nelson's Dockyard)

Location: Nelson's Dockyard, English Harbour, Antigua

Cuisine: Caribbean, International

Overview: Housed within the historic Nelson's Dockyard, The Admiral's Inn offers a unique dining experience. Patrons can enjoy a mix of Caribbean and international dishes while surrounded by the maritime charm of one of Antigua's most iconic landmarks.

7. Abracadabra Restaurant and Disco-Bar

Location: Dockyard Drive, English Harbour, Antigua

Cuisine: Italian, Caribbean Fusion

Overview: Known for its lively atmosphere, Abracadabra offers a blend of Italian and Caribbean fusion cuisine. The restaurant transforms into a vibrant disco-bar in the evenings, making it a popular spot for those seeking a dynamic dining and entertainment experience in English Harbour.

8. Le Bistro Restaurant

Location: Hodges Bay, St. John's, Antigua

Cuisine: French, Caribbean

Overview: Tucked away in Hodges Bay, Le Bistro Restaurant provides an intimate setting for those craving French and Caribbean flavors. With a focus on culinary excellence and a carefully curated wine selection, this restaurant offers a sophisticated dining experience in a tranquil location.

CHAPTER SEVEN

ENTERTAINMENT AND NIGHTLIFE

7.1 Nightclubs and Lounges with their locations

Antigua and Barbuda come alive after the sun sets, offering a vibrant nightlife scene that caters to diverse tastes. Whether you're looking to dance the night away or enjoy a more relaxed atmosphere, the islands have an array of nightclubs and lounges to explore.

1. Red Door Lounge

Location: St. John's, Antigua

Description: Situated in the heart of St. John's, the Red Door Lounge is a chic and trendy hotspot known for its stylish ambiance and eclectic music selection. With its central location, it's easily accessible for a night of dancing, socializing, and enjoying expertly crafted cocktails.

2. Abracadabra Discotheque

Location: Dockyard Drive, English Harbour, Antigua

Description: For those seeking a lively nightlife experience, Abracadabra Discotheque is a popular nightclub located in English Harbour. With a spacious dance floor, state-of-the-art lighting, and a diverse music playlist, it's a go-to destination for those looking to dance the night away in a vibrant setting.

3. Harmony Hall Jazz Club

Location: Brown's Bay, Antigua

Description: Offering a more sophisticated atmosphere, the Harmony Hall Jazz Club provides an elegant setting for live jazz performances. Situated on the picturesque Brown's Bay, this venue is perfect for those who appreciate smooth sounds, fine wines, and tapas while enjoying breathtaking views of the Caribbean Sea.

4. Pillars Bar and Restaurant

Location: Admiral's Inn, Nelson's Dockyard, English Harbour, Antigua

Description: Nestled in Nelson's Dockyard, Pillars Bar and Restaurant offers a laid-back yet stylish waterfront setting. Ideal for a relaxed evening, it provides a selection of Caribbean-inspired cocktails and a curated wine list. The outdoor terrace offers stunning views of the harbor, creating a perfect atmosphere for socializing.

5. Life Nightclub

Location: Jolly Harbour Marina, Antigua

Description: Situated in the vibrant Jolly Harbour Marina, Life Nightclub is a dynamic venue known for hosting themed parties, live performances, and international DJs. With modern décor and a lively crowd, it's a top choice for those seeking a memorable night out in a energetic and diverse atmosphere.

6. Castaways Bar

Location: Dickenson Bay, Antigua

Description: Located on the beachfront of Dickenson Bay, Castaways Bar provides a more casual and laid-back atmosphere. With an open-air setting and the soothing sound of waves, it's an ideal spot to unwind after a day of exploration, offering refreshing cocktails, local beers, and a variety of snacks.

7. Cloggy's Cafe

Location: English Harbour, Antigua

Description: Positioned in the historic English Harbour, Cloggy's Cafe is a popular lounge offering a relaxed and welcoming environment. Known for its diverse menu of cocktails and beverages, it's a great place to enjoy the evening breeze while savoring drinks and light bites in a charming Caribbean setting.

7.2 Family-Friendly Entertainment

Antigua and Barbuda provide an abundance of family-friendly entertainment options, ensuring that visitors of all ages can create lasting memories together. From engaging activities to educational experiences, the islands offer a variety of opportunities for families to bond and enjoy their time in this tropical paradise.

1. Antigua Rainforest Canopy Tour

Location: Fig Tree Drive Rainforest, Antigua

Description: An adventurous family outing awaits at the Antigua Rainforest Canopy Tour. Situated in the lush Fig Tree Drive rainforest area, this eco-friendly attraction offers a thrilling experience with ziplines and suspension bridges. It's a perfect opportunity for families to bond while enjoying the natural beauty of Antigua.

2. Stingray City

Location: Eastern Caribbean Waters, Antigua

Description: Embark on a unique marine adventure with the family at Stingray City. Gentle stingrays glide through the clear waters, providing an interactive and educational experience. Guided tours ensure a safe and enjoyable encounter, making it an exciting outing for children and adults alike.

3. Fort James

Location: St. John's Harbor, Antigua

Description: Take the family on a historical exploration at Fort James, overlooking St. John's Harbor. Children can explore the ancient ruins, learn about Antigua's colonial history, and enjoy panoramic views of the coastline. It's a blend of education and adventure, creating an engaging experience for the whole family.

4. Jolly Harbour Beach

Location: Jolly Harbour, Antigua

Description: Jolly Harbour Beach is a picturesque and family-friendly destination. The calm waters make it an ideal spot for children to swim and play, while amenities such as beachside cafes and water sports rentals add to the convenience. Families can spend a relaxing day building sandcastles and enjoying the Caribbean sunshine.

5. Antigua and Barbuda Museum

Location: St. John's, Antigua

Description: Dive into the cultural and historical heritage of Antigua and Barbuda at the Antigua and Barbuda Museum. With exhibits spanning the Amerindian era to post-independence, it offers an informative and engaging experience for families interested in the islands' rich tapestry of culture.

6. Runaway Beach

Location: St. John's, Antigua

Description: Pack a picnic and head to Runaway Beach for a day of family fun. This pristine beach, known for its soft sand and clear waters, provides an excellent backdrop for a relaxed outing. Families can swim, play beach games, and enjoy a picnic while taking in the breathtaking Caribbean scenery.

7.3 Special Events and Festivals

Antigua and Barbuda are not only known for their stunning landscapes but also for their vibrant and lively festivals and events. Throughout the year, the islands come alive with celebrations that showcase the rich cultural heritage, music, and traditions of the Caribbean. Here are some of the must-attend special events and festivals that add a unique flair to the Antiguan and Barbudan experience:

1. Antigua Sailing Week

Period: Late April to Early May

Description: Antigua Sailing Week is a world-renowned regatta that attracts sailors and sailing enthusiasts from around the globe. The event features competitive yacht races, lively parties, and a festive atmosphere in English Harbour and Falmouth Harbour, showcasing the islands' deep-rooted maritime culture.

2. Antigua Carnival

Period: Late July to Early August

Description: Antigua Carnival is a vibrant celebration of music, dance, and Caribbean culture. Festivities include lively parades, colorful costumes, steel pan performances, and soca and calypso music. The streets of St. John's come alive with energy and excitement during this annual extravaganza.

3. Independence Day Celebrations

Period: November 1st

Description: Antigua and Barbuda gained independence from British rule on November 1, 1981. Independence Day celebrations include various events such as parades, cultural performances, and patriotic displays. It's a time to witness the national pride and unity of the Antiguan and Barbudan people.

4. Barbuda Caribana

Period: June

Description: Caribana in Barbuda is an annual celebration that pays homage to the island's indigenous Carib population. The festival features traditional dance performances, cultural exhibitions, and a vibrant street parade. It provides a unique opportunity to experience the distinct heritage of Barbuda.

5. Wadadli Day

Period: November 1st

Description: Wadadli Day, celebrated on November 1st, commemorates the nation's independence. The day is marked by various cultural events and activities, including art exhibitions, live music performances, and patriotic displays. It showcases the artistic talents and cultural diversity of Antigua and Barbuda.

6. Green Castle Estate Mango Fest

Period: Late August

Description: The Green Castle Estate Mango Fest is an annual celebration held in late August. This event revolves around the abundant mango harvest and features tastings, culinary demonstrations, and live entertainment. It's a flavorful experience for food enthusiasts and a great way to savor the tropical delights of Antigua.

7. Carnival Tuesday in Barbuda

Period: June

Description: Barbuda hosts its Carnival Tuesday, a lively continuation of the Caribana celebrations. This day includes vibrant street parades, masquerade bands, and cultural performances, providing a festive atmosphere on the sister island.

7.4 Spa And Wellness Retreat

Antigua and Barbuda, with their serene landscapes and tranquil ambiance, provide an ideal setting for indulging in spa and wellness retreats. Visitors seeking relaxation, rejuvenation, and a break from the hustle and bustle of daily life will find a range of spa experiences across the islands. Here are some of the top spa and wellness retreats that promise a rejuvenating escape:

1. Blue Waters Resort and Spa

Location: North-western shore of Antigua

Description: Blue Waters Resort offers a luxurious spa experience in a tropical paradise. Surrounded by lush gardens and overlooking the Caribbean Sea, the spa provides a range of holistic treatments and therapies. It's an ideal retreat for those seeking relaxation and well-being in an exquisite setting.

2. Cocobay Resort Spa

Location: Western coast of Antigua

Description: Cocobay Resort Spa is known for its stunning views and tranquil surroundings. The spa offers a variety of treatments inspired by Caribbean traditions, promoting balance and harmony. Guests can indulge in massages with breathtaking views of the turquoise waters, creating a sensory journey for the mind and body.

3. Sandals Grande Antigua Spa

Location: Dickenson Bay, Antigua

Description: Sandals Grande Antigua boasts a world-class Red Lane Spa, providing an all-inclusive spa experience. Offering a comprehensive range of treatments, from couples massages to rejuvenating facials, the spa focuses on holistic wellness. Guests can enjoy the lush tropical surroundings while pampering themselves in a luxurious and peaceful environment.

4. Jumby Bay Island Spa

Location: Accessed by boat from Antigua

Description: Jumby Bay Island Spa provides an exclusive and secluded wellness retreat. Surrounded by pristine beaches and tropical gardens, the spa offers personalized wellness experiences, including massages, yoga, and wellness consultations. It's a haven for those seeking a private and intimate spa escape.

5. Siboney Beach Club Spa

Location: Dickenson Bay, Antigua

Description: Siboney Beach Club Spa provides a boutique spa experience with personalized services. The intimate setting and skilled therapists offer a range of treatments, from deep tissue massages to holistic therapies, ensuring a rejuvenating experience for every guest.

6. Barbuda Belle Spa

Location: Barbuda Belle Luxury Beach Hotel, Barbuda

Description: On the sister island of Barbuda, Barbuda Belle Spa at the Barbuda Belle Luxury Beach Hotel offers an exclusive wellness experience. Surrounded by pristine beaches and natural beauty, the spa focuses on holistic therapies inspired by the Caribbean environment. Guests can indulge in spa treatments with the soothing sounds of the ocean in the background.

7. Sugar Ridge Aveda Spa

Location: Sugar Ridge Resort, Jolly Harbour, Antigua

Description: The Sugar Ridge Aveda Spa, located in Jolly Harbour, offers a holistic and serene spa experience. Surrounded by lush landscapes, the spa features a range of Aveda treatments, including massages, facials, and body wraps. Guests can unwind in a tranquil environment, immersing themselves in relaxation and rejuvenation.

CHAPTER EIGHT

CULTURAL EXPERIENCES

8.1 Museums and Galleries

Museums and galleries stand as gateways to this treasure trove of stories, offering visitors a profound understanding of the vibrant past and present of this Caribbean gem.

Museum of Antigua and Barbuda: A Historical Odyssey

Situated in the heart of St. John's, the Museum of Antigua and Barbuda is a must-visit for those eager to unravel the islands' multifaceted history. Housed in the historic 18th-century Court House, the museum provides an immersive experience spanning the Amerindian settlements, the colonial era, and the journey to independence. The well-curated exhibits showcase artifacts, documents, and displays that meticulously detail the rich tapestry of Antigua and Barbuda.

Walking through the museum's corridors feels like traversing through time, with each section offering a glimpse into a different era. From the Amerindian artifacts that echo the islands' earliest inhabitants to the colonial exhibits reflecting European influence, the museum provides a chronological narrative that captivates visitors and fosters a deep appreciation for the islands' heritage.

Admiral's House Museum: Nautical Elegance in English Harbour

For those with a penchant for maritime history, the Admiral's House Museum in English Harbour provides an enchanting experience. The museum, located in the former residence of the Commander-in-Chief of the British Navy's Caribbean Fleet, immerses visitors in the naval history that has shaped Antigua and Barbuda.

Antique furniture, maritime memorabilia, and artifacts narrate tales of naval prowess and strategic importance during colonial times. The museum's setting, with its sweeping views of English Harbour, adds an extra layer of allure to the historical exploration, making it a captivating stop for both history enthusiasts and casual visitors alike.

Cedar Valley Art Studio: Where Creativity Meets Nature

Shifting gears from historical narratives to artistic expressions, the Cedar Valley Art Studio offers a different dimension of the islands' cultural richness. Nestled in a lush garden setting, this studio showcases the works of local artists who draw inspiration from the natural beauty that surrounds them.

Visitors have the opportunity to engage with artists, gaining insights into the creative process and the cultural influences that shape their work. Paintings that capture the vivid hues of Caribbean landscapes, sculptures that embody the spirit of the islands, and other forms of artistic expression converge in this space, creating an atmosphere that resonates with the vibrant soul of Antigua and Barbuda.

Exploring museums and galleries in Antigua and Barbuda not only imparts a sense of the islands' past but also connects visitors with the thriving cultural scene that defines the present. These cultural gems serve as windows into the hearts of the islands, fostering a deeper appreciation for the traditions, stories, and artistic expressions that make Antigua and Barbuda a truly enchanting destination.

8.2 Cultural Arts and Heritage

As a tourist, immersing yourself in the vibrant traditions, music, and craftsmanship will provide a deeper understanding of the local way of life.

Carnival: A Spectacle of Culture

One of the most exhilarating cultural experiences in Antigua and Barbuda is Carnival. This annual celebration, usually held in late July or early August, is a lively extravaganza that encapsulates the spirit of the islands. Carnival is a vibrant showcase of music, dance, and elaborate costumes, with the streets of St. John's coming alive with the infectious beats of steel bands and the colorful parades. Visitors are encouraged to join in the festivities, savoring the diverse rhythms of calypso, soca, and reggae, and witnessing the locals' artistic expression through their flamboyant costumes.

Antigua and Barbuda Music Festival: A Harmonious Melting Pot

For music enthusiasts, the Antigua and Barbuda Music Festival is a must-attend event. Held at various locations across the islands, this festival celebrates a diverse range of musical genres, including reggae, jazz, soca, and classical.

The festival serves as a testament to the islands' musical prowess and cultural diversity. Attending a live performance during your stay provides a unique opportunity to feel the rhythm of the Caribbean and connect with the soulful melodies that define the nation.

Crafts Market in St. John's: Artisanal Treasures

To take a piece of Antigua and Barbuda's cultural arts home with you, a visit to the Crafts Market in St. John's is essential. Here, local artisans showcase their craftsmanship, offering an array of handmade goods that reflect the islands' artistic heritage. From intricately woven baskets to vibrant batik fabrics, the market is a sensory delight. Engaging with the artists not only allows you to appreciate the skill involved but also provides an opportunity to learn about the stories and traditions woven into each piece.

Language and Local Dialects: A Linguistic Mosaic

While English is the official language of Antigua and Barbuda, visitors may encounter Antiguan Creole, a colorful linguistic blend of English, African, and Caribbean influences. Embracing the local dialect adds an extra layer to the cultural experience. Engaging in conversations with locals, learning a few phrases, or simply appreciating the melodic cadence of the language enhances your connection with the community.

Traditional Crafts and Artisanal Jewelry: Wearable Art

For those seeking tangible mementos, the islands offer a plethora of options. Handcrafted jewelry, incorporating locally sourced materials like sea glass and shells, is a popular choice. These pieces, often created by skilled artisans, capture the essence of the Caribbean and serve as wearable reminders of your cultural exploration.

8.3 Understanding Local Customs and Traditions

To truly embrace the spirit of Antigua and Barbuda, visitors are encouraged to understand and respect the local customs and traditions that shape the islands' identity. The warmth of the people and the sense of community are integral parts of the cultural fabric.

Greeting etiquette is an essential aspect of local customs. A warm smile and a friendly "Good morning" or "Good afternoon" go a long way in establishing a positive connection. Handshakes are common, and it's customary to maintain eye contact during greetings.

Respecting personal space is paramount. While the atmosphere is generally relaxed, it's important to be mindful of others' comfort zones. Whether in shops, markets, or public spaces, a polite and considerate demeanor is appreciated.

The islands' cultural diversity is reflected in the variety of languages spoken. While English is the official language, locals may converse in Antiguan Creole, a colorful blend of English, African, and Caribbean influences. Embracing this linguistic diversity adds an enriching layer to the cultural experience.

Participating in local celebrations and events is a wonderful way to immerse oneself in the traditions of Antigua and Barbuda. Whether joining a street parade during Carnival or attending a village festival, these experiences provide a firsthand glimpse into the joyous celebrations that mark significant moments in the islands' calendar.

8.4 Souvenirs and Mementos

No visit to Antigua and Barbuda is complete without taking home a piece of the islands' charm in the form of souvenirs and mementos. From traditional crafts to local delicacies, there's an array of treasures to commemorate your Caribbean adventure.

The Crafts Market in St. John's is a haven for souvenir hunters. Here, you'll find an array of handmade goods, including woven baskets, pottery, and vibrant batik fabrics. These items not only showcase the artistic prowess of the locals but also make for unique and meaningful keepsakes.

For those with a sweet tooth, the Antigua Black Pineapple is a delicious local treat. Known for its sweet and tangy flavor, this pineapple is a symbol of the islands' agricultural heritage. Visitors can indulge in pineapple jams, candies, and other delectable treats as delightful reminders of their time in Antigua.

Handcrafted jewelry, featuring locally sourced materials like sea glass and shells, is a popular choice for those seeking wearable mementos. Local artisans create stunning pieces that capture the essence of the Caribbean, making for cherished souvenirs and gifts.

Rum enthusiasts can bring a taste of Antigua and Barbuda home with a bottle of English Harbour Rum. Distilled on the islands, this award-winning rum reflects the craftsmanship and dedication to quality that defines the local spirit industry.

CHAPTER NINE

OUTDOOR ACTIVITIES

9.1 Sailing Excursions:

Embarking on a sailing excursion in Antigua and Barbuda is an immersive journey into the heart of the Caribbean's azure beauty. Whether you opt for the luxury of a private yacht or the camaraderie of a group catamaran tour, the experience promises to be nothing short of extraordinary.

Antigua, known as the "Sailing Capital of the Caribbean," boasts gentle trade winds and warm, clear waters – making it an ideal destination for sailing enthusiasts. As you set sail, the coastline unfolds like a living postcard, revealing hidden coves, pristine beaches, and lush landscapes that paint a picture of tropical paradise. The turquoise waters are a canvas for the vibrant marine life that thrives beneath the surface.

One of the highlights of a sailing excursion is the opportunity for snorkeling in these pristine waters. The crew often anchors in secluded spots near coral reefs, inviting passengers to dive into the vibrant underwater world of Cades Reef or other protected marine areas. Guided snorkeling tours reveal a kaleidoscope of colors as you encounter diverse coral formations, schools of tropical fish, and, if you're lucky, graceful rays gliding through the water. The possibility of spotting sea turtles adds an extra layer of excitement to this aquatic adventure.

Beyond the aquatic wonders, the sailing journey itself provides a sense of tranquility and freedom. The gentle rocking of the boat, the sound of waves against the hull, and the panoramic views of the horizon create a serene atmosphere. Whether you're an experienced sailor or a first-time adventurer, the skilled crews on these excursions ensure a safe and enjoyable voyage.

9.2 Zip-lining in the Rainforest:

For those seeking an adrenaline rush and a unique perspective of Antigua's natural beauty, a zip-lining adventure through the lush rainforests is an absolute must. The rainforests of Antigua offer not only a thrilling experience but also a chance to immerse yourself in the island's diverse ecosystems from a bird's-eye view.

As you soar above the treetops, the verdant canopy unfolds beneath you, revealing a tapestry of greenery and a rich tapestry of flora and fauna. The zip-lining courses are strategically designed to provide not only an exhilarating ride but also opportunities to appreciate the biodiversity of the rainforest. Experienced guides lead you through the treetops, sharing insights into the unique plant and animal life that call Antigua home.

The adventure begins with a safety briefing and equipment fitting, ensuring that even first-time zip-liners feel secure. Once harnessed, participants zip from platform to platform, navigating through the forest canopy with a sense of freedom and excitement. The varying heights and lengths of the zip lines add an element of surprise, making each leg of the journey a new and thrilling experience.

Zip-lining in Antigua is not just an adrenaline-pumping activity; it's a chance to connect with nature in a way that few experiences allow. The rush of the wind, the distant sounds of the rainforest, and the panoramic views create an unforgettable memory of the island's lush interior.

9.3 Snorkeling at Cades Reef:

Diving into the vibrant underwater world of Cades Reef is a captivating experience that combines the thrill of exploration with the serenity of being surrounded by nature's wonders. Cades Reef, a protected marine area off the coast of Antigua, is renowned for its colorful coral formations, diverse marine life, and crystal-clear waters.

Guided snorkeling tours offer a unique opportunity to immerse yourself in this underwater paradise. Before descending into the depths, experienced guides provide insights into the marine ecosystem, ensuring that even beginners feel comfortable and informed. As you glide through the water, you'll encounter an array of marine life, from schools of tropical fish weaving through the coral to elusive rays gracefully cruising along the ocean floor.

The coral formations at Cades Reef are a mesmerizing spectacle, showcasing a palette of colors and intricate structures. Snorkelers often find themselves surrounded by curious fish, each species adding its own vibrant hue to the underwater landscape. Keep your eyes peeled, and you might spot the gentle gliding of sea turtles, adding a touch of magic to the snorkeling experience.

The clear visibility and calm waters make Cades Reef an ideal location for snorkelers of all levels. Whether you're an experienced underwater enthusiast or a first-time snorkeler, the opportunity to witness the marine wonders of Antigua's waters is an experience that will stay with you long after you've left the reef behind.

9.4 Hiking to Signal Hill:

Lace up your hiking boots and set out on a trek to Signal Hill, an adventure that promises not only physical exertion but also breathtaking rewards at one of Antigua's highest points. This hiking journey takes you through lush landscapes, offering panoramic views that stretch across the island and the surrounding Caribbean Sea.

The trail to Signal Hill is a blend of natural beauty and historical significance. As you ascend, the path winds through tropical foliage, occasionally opening up to reveal vistas of the coastline below. The rich biodiversity of the island is on full display, with the calls of exotic birds providing a soundtrack to your hike.

At the summit, the reward for your efforts becomes apparent. The panoramic views are nothing short of spectacular, offering a 360-degree perspective of Antigua's diverse terrain. The turquoise waters surrounding the island contrast with the lush greenery, creating a visual masterpiece that captures the essence of the Caribbean.

Signal Hill's elevation provides an opportunity for not only scenic admiration but also a moment of reflection and connection with the natural surroundings. Whether you choose to undertake this hike at sunrise, capturing the first light over the island, or during the golden hues of sunset, the experience is bound to be unforgettable.

9.5 Kayaking in Nonsuch Bay:

Navigate the calm waters of Nonsuch Bay by embarking on a kayaking adventure through mangrove-lined channels and secluded coves. Kayaking in Nonsuch Bay provides a unique perspective, allowing you to explore the bay's natural beauty, observe local birdlife, and enjoy the serenity of this coastal haven.

Nonsuch Bay, located on the eastern coast of Antigua, is known for its tranquil waters and pristine surroundings. The bay is sheltered by a barrier reef, creating a peaceful environment that is perfect for kayaking. Whether you're a seasoned paddler or a first-time kayaker, the calm conditions make this activity accessible to all skill levels.

As you paddle through the mangrove-lined channels, keep an eye out for the diverse bird species that inhabit the area. Herons, egrets, and other coastal birds are often spotted, adding a bird-watching element to the kayaking experience. The mangroves themselves are vital ecosystems, providing shelter and breeding grounds for various marine life.

Many kayaking excursions in Nonsuch Bay include stops at secluded coves and beaches, allowing participants to take a break, swim in the clear waters, or simply bask in the natural beauty of the surroundings. Some tours also offer guided commentary on the ecology and history of the area, providing a deeper understanding of the coastal ecosystems.

Whether you choose a guided kayaking tour or opt for a self-guided exploration, kayaking in Nonsuch Bay offers a peaceful and intimate connection with Antigua's coastal treasures.

9.6 ATV Adventure on Barbuda:

For those seeking an off-road experience that combines adventure with exploration, an ATV adventure on Barbuda is a thrilling way to discover the island's diverse terrain. From sandy beaches to dense forests and scenic viewpoints, an all-terrain vehicle provides the freedom to traverse Barbuda's landscapes with ease.

Barbuda, Antigua's sister island, is less developed and known for its pristine natural beauty. An ATV adventure allows you to venture beyond the beaten path, exploring areas that may be inaccessible by traditional means. The journey takes you through sandy trails, offering a taste of the island's unique topography.

One of the highlights of the ATV adventure is the exploration of Barbuda's beaches. With miles of untouched shoreline, you can ride along the sandy stretches, feeling the wind in your hair and the warmth of the Caribbean sun on your skin. Some tours include stops at specific points of interest, such as the dramatic sea caves or hidden lagoons that dot the coastline.

As you navigate through Barbuda's interior, you'll encounter diverse landscapes, including forests and elevated vantage points that provide stunning panoramic views. The flexibility of an ATV allows you to customize your journey, ensuring you can focus on the areas of the island that intrigue you the most.

An ATV adventure on Barbuda is not just a thrilling ride; it's a chance to connect with the island's raw beauty and experience a sense of freedom as you explore its less-traveled corners. Whether you're an adrenaline enthusiast or simply seeking a unique way to discover the island, an ATV adventure promises an unforgettable experience.

CHAPTER TEN

ANTIGUA AND BARBUDA TRAVEL ITINERARIES

10.1 One-Week Highlights Tour

Day 1: Arrival in Antigua

Your adventure begins with a warm welcome to the vibrant island of Antigua. After arriving at V.C. Bird International Airport, transfer to your accommodation in the capital, St. John's. Spend the afternoon settling in and taking a leisurely stroll through the city to soak in the local atmosphere. In the evening, savor your first taste of Antiguan cuisine at a charming local restaurant.

Day 2: St. John's Exploration

Start the day with a visit to the Museum of Antigua and Barbuda, located in the heart of St. John's. Immerse yourself in the fascinating exhibits that trace the islands' history, from the indigenous people to the colonial era and beyond. After gaining insights into the cultural tapestry of Antigua, head to the bustling markets of St. John's, where local vendors showcase their crafts, spices, and fresh produce.

In the afternoon, make your way to Nelson's Dockyard, a historic naval dockyard that has been beautifully preserved. Explore the Georgian-style buildings, home to maritime museums and galleries, and stroll along the marina, soaking in the nautical atmosphere. Wrap up the day with a breathtaking sunset view from Shirley Heights, accompanied by live music and local cuisine.

Day 3: Nature and Adventure in Antigua

Embark on a scenic drive along Fig Tree Drive, winding through Antigua's lush rainforests. Take a guided hike, discovering the diverse flora and fauna while enjoying panoramic views of the island. After a morning of exploration, head to one of Antigua's pristine beaches, such as Darkwood Beach, for an afternoon of relaxation and water activities.

For a thrilling adventure, opt for a zipline experience at the Antigua Rainforest Canopy Tour. Soar through the treetops and immerse yourself in the natural beauty of the rainforest. Conclude the day with a delectable dinner at a beachfront restaurant, savoring the flavors of Caribbean cuisine.

Day 4: Sailing and Snorkeling Day

Indulge in the maritime spirit of Antigua with a full day of sailing and snorkeling. Join a sailing excursion to explore hidden coves and picturesque bays along the coastline. Snorkel in the crystal-clear waters of Cades Reef, encountering vibrant coral formations and marine life. Enjoy a delicious onboard lunch while basking in the sun and sea breeze.

In the afternoon, relax on the powdery sands of Half Moon Bay, known for its idyllic setting. Take in the stunning views and savor the tranquility of this beautiful beach. As the day comes to an end, relish a beachside dinner with the sound of the waves as your backdrop.

Day 5: Barbuda's Pink Sand Paradise

Bid farewell to Antigua as you embark on a short flight or boat journey to Barbuda. Settle into your accommodation and spend the day exploring the world-famous Pink Sand Beach. Unwind on the soft, rosy-hued sands and take a refreshing dip in the calm, turquoise waters.

As the sun begins to set, enjoy a romantic dinner at one of Barbuda's charming seaside restaurants. The intimate atmosphere and delectable seafood create a perfect evening for couples or solo travelers seeking a peaceful escape.

Day 6: Frigate Bird Sanctuary and Local Delights

Venture to the Codrington Lagoon and Frigate Bird Sanctuary, a haven for bird enthusiasts. Witness the magnificent frigate birds in their natural habitat and explore the serene surroundings of this natural reserve.

In the afternoon, immerse yourself in Barbuda's local culture by sampling traditional dishes at a local eatery. Engage with friendly locals and learn more about the island's way of life. In the evening, savor a beachfront dinner under the stars, reflecting on the unique experiences of Barbuda.

Day 7: Great Bird Island and Farewell to Paradise

Conclude your one-week highlights tour with a memorable visit to Great Bird Island. Join a boat excursion to this protected nature reserve, known for its stunning views and diverse birdlife. Hike to the island's summit for panoramic vistas and enjoy a tranquil day surrounded by nature.

As the day unfolds, indulge in a farewell lunch at a seaside restaurant, savoring the flavors of the Caribbean. In the afternoon, return to Antigua for your departure, taking with you cherished memories of a week filled with cultural discoveries, outdoor adventures, and the unparalleled beauty of Antigua and Barbuda.

10.2 Weekend Getaway

A weekend getaway to Antigua and Barbuda offers a perfect blend of relaxation, adventure, and cultural exploration. While the islands have much to offer, this itinerary is carefully curated to make the most of a short yet memorable visit.

Day 1: Arrival and St. John's Exploration

Morning:

Arrive in Antigua and head straight to the capital, St. John's. Drop your bags at your chosen accommodation and kick off your weekend adventure.

Start your exploration at the Museum of Antigua and Barbuda. Dive into the islands' rich history and cultural heritage, setting the tone for the days to come.

Afternoon:

Wander through the bustling markets of St. John's. Engage with friendly locals, sample Caribbean delicacies, and pick up unique souvenirs to remember your getaway.

Enjoy a leisurely lunch at one of the local eateries, savoring the flavors of authentic Antiguan cuisine.

Evening:

Head to Redcliffe Quay for a romantic evening stroll. The colonial architecture and vibrant atmosphere create a charming backdrop as you soak in the Caribbean ambiance.

Conclude the day with dinner at a waterfront restaurant, savoring fresh seafood and enjoying the coastal breeze.

Day 2: Coastal Adventure and Sunset Delight

Morning:

Rise early for a day of coastal exploration. Join a sailing excursion to navigate the crystal-clear waters around Antigua. Revel in the stunning views of the coastline and hidden coves.

Afternoon:

Drop anchor at one of the secluded beaches, such as Half Moon Bay. Enjoy a beach picnic and indulge in snorkeling to discover the vibrant marine life beneath the surface.

Return to St. John's in the afternoon, allowing time to relax and freshen up before the evening's activities.

Evening:

Head to Shirley Heights for a panoramic sunset experience. Sundays are particularly lively, with live music, local cuisine, and a festive atmosphere.

Capture the breathtaking sunset over English Harbour, creating memories that will linger long after your weekend escape.

Day 3: Barbuda's Pink Sands and Tranquil Waters

Morning:

Catch an early flight or boat to Barbuda, the tranquil sister island. Arrive in time to witness the morning sun casting its glow on the renowned Pink Sand Beach.

Spend the morning unwinding on the soft, rosy-hued sands, surrounded by the serenity that Barbuda is known for.

Afternoon:

Enjoy a leisurely lunch at one of the beachfront eateries, savoring the fresh catch of the day and local specialties.

Explore the Codrington Lagoon and Frigate Bird Sanctuary, a haven for bird enthusiasts. Witness the majestic frigate birds in their natural habitat.

Evening:

Conclude your weekend escape with a boat trip to Great Bird Island. Take in the breathtaking views from the island's summit and savor the tranquility of this natural reserve.

Return to Antigua in the evening, reflecting on the beauty and diversity experienced over the weekend.

10.3 Family-Friendly Adventure

Day 1: Arrival in St. John's, Antigua - Cultural Exploration

As you step off the plane onto the tropical paradise of Antigua, the excitement of your family-friendly adventure begins. Start your journey in the capital, St. John's. After checking into your family-friendly accommodation, head straight to the heart of the island's history - the Museum of Antigua and Barbuda. Engage the family with interactive exhibits that unravel the Amerindian, colonial, and post-independence eras. Take a leisurely stroll through St. John's, exploring vibrant markets where the kids can interact with locals and sample some delicious Caribbean treats. End the day with a family dinner at one of St. John's restaurants, immersing yourselves in the local culinary delights.

Day 2: Nelson's Dockyard - Maritime Marvels

On day two, delve into the maritime history of the Caribbean with a visit to Nelson's Dockyard. A UNESCO World Heritage Site, this historic naval dockyard is beautifully preserved and surrounded by Georgian-style buildings that now house museums and galleries. Explore the dockyard at your own pace, learning about the naval history and enjoying the picturesque surroundings. In the evening, head to Shirley Heights for a family-friendly sunset experience. Live music, local cuisine, and panoramic views create a festive atmosphere that everyone in the family will enjoy.

Day 3: Sailing and Snorkeling Adventure

For an exciting water-filled day, set sail on the turquoise waters of Antigua. Join a family-friendly sailing excursion that offers snorkeling opportunities at Cades Reef. Navigate through the crystal-clear waters, discovering vibrant coral formations and swimming alongside tropical fish. The day's adventure not only provides thrills but also creates lasting family memories surrounded by the beauty of the Caribbean

Sea. Return to your accommodation for a relaxed evening, reminiscing about the day's underwater discoveries.

Day 4: Flight to Barbuda - Pink Sand Paradise

On day four, take a short flight or boat trip to Barbuda, known for its family-friendly atmosphere and pristine beaches. Upon arrival, head straight to the renowned Pink Sand Beach, a picture-perfect setting for a family day by the sea. Let the kids build sandcastles, splash in the shallow waters, and enjoy the serene surroundings. As the sun sets, create a memorable family evening by the beach, perhaps with a beachside picnic or a barbecue.

Day 5: Codrington Lagoon and Frigate Bird Sanctuary - Nature Exploration

Explore Barbuda's natural wonders on day five with a visit to the Codrington Lagoon and Frigate Bird Sanctuary. This educational outing allows the whole family to witness the majesty of frigate birds in their natural habitat. Board a boat to navigate the lagoon, learning about the significance of this sanctuary in preserving Barbuda's unique ecosystem. In the afternoon, let the kids enjoy some free time on Pink Sand Beach while you relax and take in the tranquil atmosphere.

Day 6: Great Bird Island - Wildlife Discovery

Embark on a family-friendly boat trip to Great Bird Island, a protected nature reserve. This day promises adventure and wildlife spotting, making it an ideal family activity. Hike to the island's summit for breathtaking views, and keep an eye out for the diverse bird species inhabiting the area. Return to

Barbuda's Pink Sand Beach for a relaxing evening, perhaps enjoying a family dinner at one of the beachside restaurants.

Day 7: Return to Antigua - Adventure Continues

Bid farewell to Barbuda as you return to Antigua for the final leg of your family-friendly adventure. Spend the day exploring historic sites like Fort James, providing both education and entertainment for the family. For an added adrenaline rush, embark on an ATV adventure to uncover hidden gems and enjoy the thrill of off-road exploration. Conclude the day with a family dinner, sharing stories and reliving the highlights of your Antigua and Barbuda family adventure.

Day 8: Darkwood Beach - Family Beach Day

On your last full day in Antigua, dedicate some quality family time to Darkwood Beach. Known for its calm waters, this beach is perfect for swimming, building sandcastles, and enjoying the picturesque surroundings. Pack a picnic and spend the day relaxing by the sea, creating cherished memories with the family. As the sun sets on your family-friendly adventure, indulge in a farewell dinner at a beachfront restaurant, savoring the flavors of the Caribbean.

Day 9: Departure - Carrying Memories Home

As you bid farewell to Antigua and Barbuda, take with you the memories of a family-friendly adventure filled with cultural exploration, outdoor activities, and moments of pure relaxation. The islands have woven a tapestry of experiences that catered to every member of the family, creating a vacation that will be remembered for years to come. Until the next family adventure, Antigua and Barbuda will linger in your hearts as a tropical haven that welcomed you with open arms and left you with a treasure trove of family memories.

10.4 Solo Traveler's Journey

Day 1: Arrival in St. John's

Arrive in St. John's, the capital of Antigua, and settle into your chosen accommodation. As a solo traveler, you may opt for a cozy guesthouse or boutique hotel, providing a personalized and immersive experience.

Begin your journey with a leisurely stroll through St. John's, absorbing the lively atmosphere of the capital. Explore the local markets, where vendors display vibrant crafts and fresh produce. Engage with the friendly locals and sample some of the delicious Caribbean street food.

In the evening, head to a waterfront restaurant to enjoy a quiet dinner while watching the sunset over the Caribbean Sea. This sets the tone for your solo adventure, offering a sense of tranquility and anticipation for the days ahead.

Day 2: Cultural Immersion

Dive into the cultural treasures of Antigua with a visit to the Museum of Antigua and Barbuda. Explore the exhibits at your own pace, gaining insights into the islands' history, from Amerindian settlements to colonial influences and the journey to independence.

After the museum, wander through the historic streets of St. John's, where colorful colonial-era buildings stand as a testament to the island's past. Take in the unique blend of

European and Caribbean influences, capturing the essence of Antigua's cultural diversity.

For the evening, consider a visit to a local bar or pub, where you can interact with fellow travelers and perhaps make new connections. Embrace the social aspect of solo travel, sharing stories and experiences with like-minded individuals.

Day 3: Nelson's Dockyard and Sunset Serenity

On day three, venture to Nelson's Dockyard, a UNESCO World Heritage Site located in English Harbour. Explore the beautifully preserved naval dockyard and its surroundings, delving into the maritime history of the Caribbean.

In the afternoon, take a scenic drive or hike to Shirley Heights, an iconic viewpoint overlooking English Harbour. Sundays at Shirley Heights are particularly special, featuring live music, local cuisine, and a vibrant sunset celebration. It's an excellent opportunity to connect with both locals and fellow travelers.

Day 4: Journey to Barbuda

Bid farewell to Antigua as you embark on a short flight or boat trip to Barbuda. As a solo traveler, Barbuda offers a serene and intimate retreat. Choose accommodation that aligns with your preference for solitude, perhaps opting for a beachfront cottage or a cozy guesthouse.

Spend the afternoon unwinding on the famous Pink Sand Beach, where the soft, rosy-hued sands provide a picturesque setting for relaxation. Enjoy the tranquility of Barbuda, immersing yourself in the calming sounds of the ocean.

Day 5: Codrington Lagoon and Frigate Bird Sanctuary

Explore the natural wonders of Barbuda with a visit to the Codrington Lagoon and Frigate Bird Sanctuary. This protected area is home to a significant population of frigate birds, offering a unique opportunity for birdwatching and connecting with nature.

Take a boat trip through the lagoon, appreciating the diverse ecosystem and the majestic presence of frigate birds soaring above. This day provides a peaceful yet captivating experience, allowing for moments of solitude amidst the untouched beauty of Barbuda.

Day 6: Great Bird Island Exploration

Embark on a solo boat trip to Great Bird Island, a protected nature reserve off the coast of Barbuda. This intimate adventure offers opportunities for hiking, exploring, and connecting with the island's natural surroundings.

Climb to the summit of Great Bird Island for panoramic views of the Caribbean Sea, providing a breathtaking backdrop for moments of self-reflection. Enjoy a picnic on the beach or simply savor the solitude of this secluded paradise.

Day 7: Reflecting on Paradise

As your solo journey nears its end, spend the final day in Barbuda indulging in personal reflections. Return to Pink Sand Beach for a leisurely day of relaxation, absorbing the tranquil atmosphere and appreciating the simplicity of the surroundings.

Take a quiet walk along the shoreline, allowing the sound of the waves and the gentle breeze to accompany your thoughts. Capture the moments of solitude and natural beauty that define Barbuda's essence.

Day 8: Farewell to Antigua

Return to Antigua for the last leg of your solo adventure. Reflect on the experiences gained, connections made, and the sense of independence cultivated during your time in Antigua and Barbuda.

Consider a visit to Devil's Bridge, a natural limestone arch on the eastern coast of Antigua. The dramatic landscapes provide a fitting backdrop for contemplation and self-reflection as you bid farewell to this Caribbean paradise.

Conclude your solo journey with a quiet dinner at a seaside restaurant, reminiscing about the memories created and the personal growth achieved throughout your exploration of Antigua and Barbuda. As you depart, carry with you the unique and enriching experiences that only a solo journey can provide.

10.5 Romantic Getaways

Day 1: Arrival in Romantic St. John's

Your romantic getaway in Antigua and Barbuda begins with your arrival in the capital city, St. John's. After settling into your chosen accommodation, take a leisurely stroll through the cobblestone streets of the city, hand in hand. Explore the charming markets of St. John's, where local vendors showcase vibrant crafts and delectable treats. As evening descends, head to a waterfront restaurant to indulge in a candlelit dinner, savoring the first tastes of the Caribbean's culinary delights.

Day 2: Immersive Cultural Experience

Begin your second day with a visit to the Museum of Antigua and Barbuda, situated in the heart of St. John's. Delve into the islands' rich history, learning about the Amerindian heritage, colonial era, and post-independence developments. The intimate setting of the museum provides a serene start to your romantic journey, offering moments of connection and shared exploration.

In the afternoon, head to Nelson's Dockyard, a UNESCO World Heritage Site. Wander through the historic naval dockyard, surrounded by beautifully restored colonial buildings. This iconic site not only presents a glimpse into the Caribbean's maritime history but also provides a tranquil backdrop for romantic moments. As the sun sets, make your way to Shirley Heights for a panoramic view of English Harbour. Sundays offer a particularly enchanting atmosphere with live music and local cuisine.

Day 3: Barbuda Bound for Seclusion

On the third day, take a short flight or boat trip to Barbuda, a haven for romance-seekers. Upon arrival, you'll be captivated by the secluded beauty of Pink Sand Beach. Spend your day lounging on the soft, rosy-hued sands, enjoying each other's company amidst the serene surroundings. The tranquil atmosphere of Barbuda sets the perfect stage for intimate moments and shared bliss.

Day 4: Birdwatching and Beachside Bliss

Embark on a boat trip to the Codrington Lagoon and Frigate Bird Sanctuary, a unique experience for nature-loving couples. Witness the elegance of frigate birds in their natural habitat, fostering a connection with the incredible wildlife of the region. After this immersive encounter, return to Pink Sand Beach for a romantic evening by the water, complete with a sunset walk along the shoreline.

Day 5: Private Exploration of Great Bird Island

On your fifth day, opt for a private boat trip to Great Bird Island. This secluded nature reserve offers a romantic setting for exploration and connection. Hike to the island's summit hand in hand, taking in the breathtaking views. Enjoy a picnic on the pristine beaches, savoring the seclusion and tranquility of this intimate getaway.

Day 6: Return to Romantic Antigua

Bid farewell to the blissful tranquility of Barbuda and return to Antigua for the second leg of your romantic journey. Spend the afternoon at Darkwood Beach, a serene stretch of shoreline known for its calm waters. Enjoy a leisurely day by the sea, basking in the romance of the Caribbean sun.

Day 7: Sailing and Snorkeling Adventure

Immerse yourselves in a day of adventure with a private sailing excursion along Antigua's coastline. Discover hidden coves, secluded beaches, and crystal-clear waters together. Engage in snorkeling activities, exploring the vibrant underwater world hand in hand. As the sun sets on your penultimate day, reflect on the memories created during this romantic escapade.

Day 8: Devil's Bridge and Culinary Delights

Visit Devil's Bridge on the eastern coast of Antigua for a reflective and contemplative morning. The natural limestone arch offers a unique backdrop for shared moments of connection. In the afternoon, indulge in a culinary adventure, exploring the diverse flavors of local cuisine at one of Antigua's waterfront restaurants. Allow the Caribbean breeze to enhance the romantic ambiance as you savor each bite.

Day 9: Private Dinner and Serenity at Hermitage Bay

On your ninth day, elevate the romance with a private dinner at a secluded spot overlooking the ocean. Many resorts and beachfront restaurants offer personalized dining experiences, creating an intimate atmosphere under the starlit Caribbean sky. Conclude your romantic getaway with a relaxing day at Hermitage Bay, a luxurious beachfront setting perfect for couples seeking serenity and shared moments of bliss.

As you bid farewell to Antigua and Barbuda, carry with you the memories of a romantic journey filled with cultural exploration, intimate moments, and the serene beauty of the Caribbean islands. Your getaway has not only deepened your connection but also left an indelible mark of romance on these picturesque islands.

Note: Depending on your travel goals as stated in chapter one of this travel guide and the type of travel itinerary you would like to go for, you can still add some places you would like to visit which were not included in your choice travel itinerary, you can adjust any of them to suit your travel goals so as to a have an enjoyable and memorable trip.

ELEVEN

PRACTICAL TIPS AND RESOURCES

11.1 Local Phrases and Vocabulary

As you embark on your journey to Antigua and Barbuda, it's advantageous to familiarize yourself with some local phrases and vocabulary. While English is the official language, the islands boast a unique blend of expressions and colloquialisms that reflect the rich cultural tapestry. Engaging with these phrases not only enhances your travel experience but also endears you to the warm and friendly locals.

Greetings and Courtesies:

- "Wah gwan?" - A casual greeting meaning "What's going on?" or "How are you?"
- "Good morning/afternoon/evening" - Standard English greetings but widely used and appreciated.
- "Mi deh yah" - Locals saying "I'm here," expressing their presence in a friendly manner.

Expressions of Appreciation:

- "Big up!" - A shout-out or expression of admiration for something impressive.
- "Wicked!" - Used to describe something exceptionally good or cool.

- "Thanks a million" - A heartfelt way to express gratitude.

Food and Drinks:

- "Nyam" - To eat with gusto. You might hear locals saying, "Let's nyam some delicious local dishes."
- "Wash down" - To enjoy food with a beverage, often used when having a meal.

Getting Around:

- "Wha gwaan pon de road?" - What's happening on the road? A friendly way to ask about the latest news or events.
- "Link up" - Make plans to meet up or connect with someone.

Time and Punctuality:

- "Soon come" - A relaxed approach to time, meaning arriving shortly or in due course.
- "Island time" - Refers to the laid-back, easygoing pace of life on the islands.

11.2 Emergency Contacts

While Antigua and Barbuda are generally safe destinations for travelers, it's essential to be aware of emergency contacts to ensure your well-being throughout your stay.

1. Police:

In case of any emergency or if you need police assistance, dial 911. The police force in Antigua and Barbuda is responsive and well-trained to handle various situations.

2. Medical Emergencies:

For medical emergencies, contact the Mount St. John's Medical Centre at (268) 484-2700. This hospital is well-equipped to provide quality medical care to residents and visitors alike.

3. Fire and Rescue:

In the event of a fire or other emergencies requiring rescue services, dial 911. The fire department in Antigua and Barbuda is prompt and well-prepared to handle emergencies.

4. Embassy Contacts:

If you're a foreign visitor, it's advisable to have your country's embassy or consulate contact information handy. In case of lost passports, legal issues, or other consular services, your embassy can provide valuable assistance.

11.3 Sustainable Travel Practices

Antigua and Barbuda are committed to sustainable tourism practices to preserve the natural beauty and cultural heritage of the islands. As a responsible traveler, you can contribute to these efforts by adopting eco-friendly habits during your visit.

1. Respect Local Ecosystems:

Explore natural attractions with care, staying on designated paths and avoiding disturbance to wildlife. Coral reefs, mangroves, and national parks are vital to the islands' ecosystems and should be treated with respect.

2. Reduce, Reuse, Recycle:

Limit your use of single-use plastics, and dispose of waste responsibly. Many accommodations and attractions on the islands actively promote recycling, and participating in these initiatives helps minimize environmental impact.

3. Support Local Businesses:

Opt for locally-owned hotels, restaurants, and shops to contribute directly to the community. This ensures that a more significant portion of your spending stays within the local economy, fostering sustainable development.

4. Conserve Water and Energy:

Given the islands' reliance on desalination for freshwater, be mindful of your water usage. Additionally, conserve energy by turning off lights, air conditioning, and other electronic devices when not in use.

5. Educate Yourself:

Learn about the islands' environmental challenges and conservation efforts. Understanding the local context allows you to make informed choices that align with sustainable travel principles.

11.4 Health Precautions

Ensuring your health and well-being during your stay in Antigua and Barbuda is paramount. While the islands are generally safe, it's essential to take necessary health precautions to fully enjoy your trip.

1. Vaccinations and Health Insurance:

Ensure that your routine vaccinations are up-to-date before traveling. Additionally, consider vaccinations for diseases like Hepatitis A and B. Travel insurance with comprehensive health coverage is recommended for unforeseen medical emergencies.

2. Safe Food and Water Practices:

To prevent food and waterborne illnesses, stick to bottled or purified water and avoid consuming raw or undercooked seafood. Ensure that fruits and vegetables are thoroughly washed and peeled before consumption.

3. Insect Protection:

Protect yourself from mosquito bites, especially during dawn and dusk, to minimize the risk of mosquito-borne diseases such as Zika, dengue, and chikungunya. Use insect repellent and wear long sleeves and pants in areas where mosquitoes are prevalent.

4. Sun Safety:

The Caribbean sun can be intense. Use sunscreen with a high SPF, wear sunglasses and a wide-brimmed hat, and seek shade during peak sun hours to prevent sunburn and heat-related illnesses.

5. Medical Facilities and Medications:

Know the location of medical facilities on the islands, and carry a basic first aid kit. If you require prescription medications, bring an ample supply and ensure you have the necessary documentation for travel.

6. COVID-19 Precautions:

Stay informed about the latest COVID-19 guidelines and travel restrictions. Adhere to local regulations, practice good hygiene, and respect social distancing measures to protect yourself and others.

By following these health precautions, you can ensure a safe and enjoyable experience in Antigua and Barbuda. Remember that your well-being is a priority, and taking proactive steps enhances your overall travel experience.

CONCLUSION

Appendix: Additional Resources

As you conclude your journey through the pages of this Antigua and Barbuda Travel Guide, consider the following additional resources to enhance your understanding and appreciation of these Caribbean gems:

1. Online Travel Communities:

For continuous inspiration and real-time advice, engage with vibrant online travel communities dedicated to Antigua and Barbuda. Platforms like TripAdvisor bring together a wealth of firsthand experiences, travel tips, and up-to-date recommendations from fellow explorers. Dive into discussion forums, read reviews on accommodations, and seek insights on the latest local happenings. Connecting with the online travel community not only enhances your trip preparation but also allows you to share your unique experiences, contributing to the collective tapestry of Antigua and Barbuda travel narratives. Remember, the virtual camaraderie of these platforms can extend the joy of your Caribbean adventure well beyond the shores of the islands.

2. Local Tourism Offices:

Engaging with the local tourism offices in Antigua and Barbuda is a valuable resource for enhancing your travel experience. The Antigua and Barbuda Tourism Authority serves as a hub for up-to-date information on events, attractions, and any travel advisories. The friendly and knowledgeable staff can provide personalized recommendations, maps, and brochures to ensure you make the most of your visit. Whether seeking insider tips on hidden gems, guidance on cultural events, or assistance with practicalities, the tourism offices are your go-to source. Visit their website or drop by their physical locations to tap into the wealth of knowledge these offices offer, ensuring a seamless and enriched exploration of the twin islands.

3. Books and Literature:

Delve into the captivating narratives that illuminate the rich history and cultural tapestry of Antigua and Barbuda. Start with Jamaica Kincaid's poignant "A Small Place," a powerful exploration of the island's colonial legacy and the complexities of identity. For a historical perspective, "Antigua, Penny, Puce" by Robert B. Hill offers a detailed account of Antiguan history. Immerse yourself in the Caribbean charm through "The Star-Apple Kingdom" by Derek Walcott, a Nobel laureate whose poetry beautifully captures the spirit of the islands. These literary gems provide a deeper understanding of Antigua and Barbuda, enriching your travel experience with the insights and perspectives of seasoned storytellers.

4. Documentaries and Films:

Immerse yourself further in the allure of Antigua and Barbuda by exploring captivating documentaries and films that showcase the islands' beauty and cultural richness. For a visual journey, consider watching "This Caribbean Life," a documentary series providing an intimate look into the daily lives of locals and the vibrant traditions that define Antiguan and Barbudan culture. Additionally, the film "Island in the Sun" captures the breathtaking landscapes, offering a cinematic experience that transports you to the heart of the Caribbean. These visual narratives not only complement your travel experience but also deepen your appreciation for the history, traditions, and natural wonders that make Antigua and Barbuda a truly unique destination.

5. Language Resources:

Immerse yourself in the vibrant local culture of Antigua and Barbuda by delving into the islands' unique linguistic tapestry. While English is the official language, Antiguan Creole and Barbudan dialects add a colorful flair to everyday conversations. To enhance your linguistic experience, consider language resources that offer insights into these captivating dialects. A helpful starting point is the "Antiguan and Barbudan Creole" phrasebook, which provides key expressions and local nuances. Embrace the opportunity to connect with locals on a deeper level by incorporating a few phrases into your interactions. Language resources not only facilitate communication but also foster a richer understanding of the islands' cultural nuances, creating moments of genuine connection during your Antigua and Barbuda adventure.

Final Thoughts and Recommendations

As you reach the end of this travel guide, let the memories of your Antigua and Barbuda adventure linger like the warmth of the Caribbean sun on your skin. Reflect on the diversity of experiences – from historical explorations to thrilling outdoor adventures, from culinary delights to cultural connections. Antigua and Barbuda have offered you more than just a vacation; they have woven themselves into the fabric of your travel story.

In your reflections, consider the moments that stood out, the lessons learned, and the connections made. As you carry the spirit of these islands with you, remember that your journey doesn't end here; it becomes a part of your personal narrative, a chapter to revisit in your travel chronicles.

Should you find yourself yearning for more Caribbean adventures or exploring new horizons, may this guide serve as a companion, offering inspiration and practical insights. Your Antigua and Barbuda adventure is a testament to the beauty of travel – the ability to discover, connect, and carry a piece of the world with you wherever you go.

Safe travels, fellow adventurer, and may your future journeys be as enriching and vibrant as the time you spent in the heart of Antigua and Barbuda.

Made in the USA
Las Vegas, NV
22 November 2024